Becoming a Physiotherapist

Is Physiotherapy Really the Career for You?

First edition

Chris McKenna and Cath Wright

First edition March 2017
ISBN 9781 5097 0762 1
e-ISBN 9781 5097 0766 9
e-ISBN 9781 5097 0770 6

British Library Cataloguing-in-Publication Data
A catalogue record for this book is available from the British Library

Published by
BPP Learning Media Ltd
BPP House, Aldine Place
London W12 8AA

www.bpp.com/health

Printed in the United Kingdom by
RICOH UK Limited
Unit 2
Wells Place
Merstham
RH1 3LG

> Your learning materials, published by BPP Learning Media Ltd, are printed on paper sourced from sustainable, managed forests.

All rights reserved. No part of this publication may be reproduced, stored in a retrieval system or transmitted in any form or by any means, electronic, mechanical, photocopying, recording or otherwise, without the prior written permission of BPP Learning Media.

The views expressed in this book are those of BPP Learning Media and not those of UCAS or any universities. BPP Learning Media are in no way associated with or endorsed by UCAS or any universities.

The contents of this book are intended as a guide and not professional advice. Although every effort has been made to ensure that the contents of this book are correct at the time of going to press, BPP Learning Media, the Editor and the Author make no warranty that the information in this book is accurate or complete and accept no liability for any loss or damage suffered by any person acting or refraining from acting as a result of the material in this book.

Every effort has been made to contact the copyright holders of any material reproduced within this publication. If any have been inadvertently overlooked, BPP Learning Media will be pleased to make the appropriate credits in any subsequent reprints or editions.

© BPP School of Health 2017

A note about copyright

Dear Customer

What does the little © mean and why does it matter?

Your market-leading BPP books, course materials and e-learning materials do not write and update themselves. People write them on their own behalf or as employees of an organisation that invests in this activity. Copyright law protects their livelihoods. It does so by creating rights over the use of the content.

Breach of copyright is a form of theft – as well as being a criminal offence in some jurisdictions, it is potentially a serious beach of professional ethics.

With current technology, things might seem a bit hazy but, basically, without the express permission of BPP Learning Media:

- Photocopying our materials is a breach of copyright

- Scanning, ripcasting or conversion of our digital materials into different file formats, uploading them to facebook or e-mailing them to your friends is a breach of copyright

You can, of course, sell your books, in the form in which you have bought them – once you have finished with them. (Is this fair to your fellow students? We update for a reason.) But the e-products are sold on a single user license ba sis: we do not supply 'unlock' codes to people who have bought them secondhand.

And what about outside the UK? BPP Learning Media strives to make our materials available at prices students can afford by local printing arrangements, pricing policies and partnerships which are clearly listed on our website. A tiny minority ignore this and indulge in criminal activity by illegally photocopying our material or supporting organisations that do. If they act illegally and unethically in one area, can you really trust them?

Contents

About the publisher	vii
About the authors	vii
Foreword	viii
Acknowledgements	ix
Shining a light on your future career path	x

1 Introduction and overview — 1

2 How do I know that physiotherapy is the right career for me? — 7

What do you want from your career?	9
Can someone with a disability be a physiotherapist?	10
What are the qualities of a good physiotherapist?	11
Personal skills	11
Academic skills	11
Practical skills	12
What relevant experience should I get?	12
Working in a team	13
Understanding and communicating with people	14

3 How do I choose which course and university to apply to? — 19

Location – does it matter?	21
Should I live at home?	23
What courses are available?	24
Postgraduate or undergraduate?	25
Should I worry about reputation?	27
What is the course structure?	28
How do they teach and how do I learn?	29
How will I be assessed?	30

4	**How do I apply?**	33
	The Universities and Colleges Admission System (UCAS)	35
	Direct application	36
	What do the admissions team look for?	36
	Your personal statement	36
	The interview process	38
	Individual interviews	38
	Group interviews	38
	Group activities	39
	Feedback	40
	What if I still have questions?	41
5	**What is life like as a student?**	45
	Accommodation	47
	Living in student halls	47
	Living in a shared house	47
	Renting a room	48
	Finance	48
	Timetables	48
	Books and equipment	49
	Induction week	51
	Library facilities	52
	University support	53
	Academic support	53
	Financial support	53
	Counselling services	54
	Personal tutors	54
	Extra-curricular activities	56
	The students' union and the Chartered Society of Physiotherapy	56
6	**How do I manage my finances as a student?**	61
	Accommodation costs	64
	Are there professional costs related to my course?	65
	Will I have to pay fees?	66
	Can I obtain a student loan?	66
	Special needs funding application	68

7	**What do the early years of studying physiotherapy involve?**	71
	What skills can I transfer to the programme?	73
	Do I need to be practical or academic?	74
	Topics covered	75
	Anatomy and physiology	75
	Physiotherapy assessment, intervention and evaluation	76
	Research	76
	Practice placement	77
	Getting the most out of lectures	78
	Getting the most out of seminars	79
	Getting the most out of practical/laboratory classes	81
	Other learning opportunities	81
8	**Physiotherapy practice placements**	83
	What does being on practice placement mean?	85
	What activities will I undertake?	86
	What hours will I work?	87
	Do I wear uniform?	87
	Will I get support?	88
	How will I be assessed?	89
	What about my safety?	91
	What is an elective placement?	92
	Is there an opportunity to study overseas?	93
9	**What do the final years of studying physiotherapy involve?**	95
	Is there a dissertation to write?	97
	Will there be option modules?	99
	Preparing for practice	100
	Developing a continuous professional development (CPD) portfolio	101
	Final exams	103
	The National Student Survey and the Postgraduate Taught Experience Survey	103

10 What career paths are available to me? 107

Getting your first job 109
Starting your own business 111
Registering with the Health and Care Professions Council (HCPC) 111
Joining your professional body 112
Professional indemnity 113
Preceptorship and mentorship 113
The NHS Knowledge and Skills Framework (KSF) 114
Choosing a speciality 114
Becoming a consultant physiotherapist 115
Taking the management path 115
Thinking about teaching 117
Working internationally 118

11 Physiotherapy in the statutory sector 121

The National Health Service (NHS) 123
Inter-professional working 128

12 Physiotherapy in the non-statutory sector 131

New areas of independent practice 138

13 International perspectives 141

14 A day in the life – physiotherapy in action 149

Index 161

About the publisher

The UK's only university solely dedicated to business and the professions.

We are dedicated to preparing you for a professional career. We offer a strong commercial approach, within a business culture designed to help you stand out in the workplace after you graduate. Our programmes are designed in partnership with employers and respected professionals in the fields of law, business, finance and health.

About the authors

Chris McKenna is a Senior Fellow of the Higher Education Academy and a programme leader in the School of Health & Social Care at Teesside University. He has interviewed potential students for over 15 years. Chris has taught inter-professionally for over 20 years. Current areas of interest are based around sensory profiling with children who have additional study needs.

Cath Wright is a Senior Fellow of the Higher Education Academy and a senior lecturer and admissions tutor at Teesside University. She has had experience in a wide variety of practice areas and had responsibility for a range of inter-professional teams. Her interests lie within leadership and service development and her current research is in the area of co-dependence.

Foreword

This is the book I wish had been available to me when I started thinking about becoming a physiotherapist and then again when I actually commenced training; it demystifies the profession as well as provides a route map through the extensive resources available to you. It challenges the assumptions you may have about the profession and opens your mind to its many diversities.

Choosing physiotherapy as a career was simply one of the best decisions I have ever made as it is a profession that just keeps on giving; it has enabled me to work in a whole range of environments, to teach, to travel, to manage and to lead but, most importantly, it has enabled me to make a difference to people's lives which is why I wanted to come into the profession in the first place. The options and choices that are now available about routes into training and your career path are even more extensive now so a book like this is invaluable in guiding you through.

The more you are prepared to invest in your chosen profession, the greater the reward and the Chartered Society of Physiotherapy will be with you every step of the way from before you start your training, right through, and including, your retirement. We look forward to welcoming you!

Professor Karen Middleton CBE FCSP MA
Chief Executive, The Chartered Society of Physiotherapy
Visiting Professor, Leeds Beckett University

Acknowledgements

We would like to thank all of our colleagues, students and physiotherapists who have contributed case studies and insights for this book so generously. We would like to thank Dave Grover, Steven Barr and Dan Spence for their assistance in reviewing this book. Their specialist knowledge has been invaluable. Thanks also to Abbie Davies for her creative input.

Cath is grateful to Mark, Amy and Adam for all their encouragement and to the many physiotherapists who have contributed to the content of this book.

From Chris – Thank you to my sweetheart, Rachel, and my children – Isaac, Jemima, Abel and Isabella for the patience and support that allows me to go to work each day. To all the physiotherapists I have worked with and who have inspired me over the years a heartfelt thanks. Your work reminds me that what we do makes a difference.

Shining a light on your future career path

The process of researching and identifying a career that you are most suited to can be a somewhat daunting process, but the rewards of following a career that truly engages you should not be underestimated. Deciding on your future career path should be viewed as a fun and extremely satisfying process that, if done correctly, will benefit you greatly.

Carefully considering a short list of future career options and what each one will offer you will help you to make a truly informed decision. Although it is perfectly acceptable to change career direction at a later date, reviewing the options open to you now will help to ensure that you are satisfied with your career from the outset.

I first began mentoring aspiring professionals ten years ago when it was clear that many individuals were not gaining access to the careers guidance they required. It was with this in mind that I embarked on publishing our *Becoming a* series of books, to provide help, support and clear insight into career choices. I hope that this book will help you to make an informed decision as to what career you are most suited to, your strengths and your aspirations.

I would like to take this opportunity to wish you the very best of luck with identifying your future career and hope that you pass on some of the gems of wisdom that you acquire along the way, to those who follow in your footsteps.

Matt Green
Series Editor – *Becoming a* series
Director of Professional Development
BPP University

Chapter 1

Introduction and overview

This book provides direction to help you make an informed decision about your future as a physiotherapist. Choosing a career is a difficult process and this book will help to make that decision easier. You may be considering attending university for the first time or perhaps returning to university. This will bring about great change for you, whatever your situation; decisions about leaving home, changing career and choosing the right course are all very important at this time and this book will discuss the options available to you.

While much of the content relates to the general university experience in the UK the main focus throughout is the study of physiotherapy itself. Many of the frequently asked questions about physiotherapy education are answered and where this has not been possible you will be directed to the best place to locate this information. This book provides answers to the sorts of questions you need to consider before deciding if physiotherapy is for you.

There are a number of areas which potential students find confusing. In Chapter 3 consideration is given to the level of study and the manner of delivery of the course material. You will be given information about the kinds of assessment you might expect to undertake as well as information to help you choose a university appropriate to your personal circumstances. The application process is considered in Chapter 4, including what the admissions team will be looking for in your personal statement and at interview. Your expectations of life as a student may have been generated by the anecdotes of others and reports in the media. Here you will find an objective viewpoint. Chapter 5 includes information about finance, equipment, the potential facilities and support offered at university. As finance is one of the major considerations for any new student, this area of potential stress is also explored in Chapter 6.

The mystery of what you will actually study has been broken down in Chapter 7 and Chapter 9. The content of curricula has been uncovered to give you an insight into the main areas of study and how the early learning provides an underpinning for later study. These chapters are separated by Chapter 8 which considers the practice placement element of the course. This is often the element of the programme which students most enjoy. The variety of placements available is discussed, including the concept of non-traditional placements.

Physiotherapists use a range of approaches to help people maintain their health. Those who pursue a career in physiotherapy should already understand the importance of the profession in effecting change in the lives of service users and their carers. In Chapter 11 and Chapter 12 the different opportunities for physiotherapists to practise in once they have graduated are investigated. It is not possible to cover every area of practice due to the extensive range of existing roles and the continuous development of new practice areas. Some consideration has been given to potential practice roles and a series of case studies has been included to illustrate some of the existing roles of the physiotherapist. The book provides a reminder in Chapter 13 that physiotherapists are part of an international profession with international links and responsibilities. It introduces you to the World Confederation for Physical Therapy, and the current international agenda.

Chapter 14 closes the book with a series of narratives. Each explores a real day in the life of a physiotherapist. These stories help you appreciate the reality of practice and provide a flavour of the opportunities which await a practitioner.

You are at the threshold of a new and exciting career.

Case study: Why I chose to do physiotherapy – Sunu Mammen

Physiotherapy provided me with the opportunity to be part of a health profession that had a role in educating patients about their lifestyle, as well as treating the conditions they presented with. A holistic approach was the focus of any care for me, and physiotherapy seemed to always advocate this. The more I researched into the role of the physiotherapist in the hospital, and the wider community, the more I was drawn to the profession. Once I started the course everything I had studied came alive on practice placements. To see the progression of patients during and after rehabilitation with the physiotherapist and a wider team provided complete job satisfaction. This course has allowed me to develop so many skills, as well as an insight into my own strengths and weaknesses. The support provided by the university and fellow students has made my university experience very pleasant. As I complete the final year, I am very proud to be part of this profession. I am also very glad I made the choice to follow this career, and am excited to see what the future holds.

People will commence their training for their own reasons and this book will serve you well as a resource throughout your training and beyond. It will give focus and direction to your personal research and should enable you to confidently select an appropriate programme, submit a more relevant application and prepare for an interview. This book has been designed to help you succeed in the career of your choice. The questions it answers and the ideas raised will help facilitate that success. The rest is up to you.

Chapter summary

Physiotherapy may be your first choice of career. That decision will have been guided by a set of your own, very personal circumstances. Others will have made a similar decision in the past and have pursued very fulfilling careers. As you embark on a journey to become a physiotherapist you will develop skills and gain great knowledge of the profession until you can walk across the stage at graduation to applause from friends and family; from there you will enter your first post in what will be a rewarding and successful career.

Key points

- You should do plenty of research before deciding on a career in physiotherapy.
- Think about what you want to get out of your career.
- Think about what you want to study, where you want to study and how you want to study.
- Make sure you gain a good understanding of the profession in a range of different settings.
- Reflect on why you want to be a physiotherapist.

Useful resources

The Chartered Society of Physiotherapy: www.csp.org.uk

NHS Careers: www.nhscareers.nhs.uk

Chapter 2

How do I know that physiotherapy is the right career for me?

> **Definition**
>
> Physiotherapy helps to restore movement and function when someone is affected by injury, illness or disability. (CSP, 2013)

Physiotherapists use a range of approaches to help people maintain their health. This may be with individuals affected by injury or illness or to help their patients manage pain or prevent disease. This might require the physiotherapist to provide advice about strategies to improve the way that people complete daily tasks such as lifting; they may provide specialised exercises to strengthen specific parts of the body and improve general health. The physiotherapist might also help to relieve pain and stiffness by using their hands in manual therapy.

Physiotherapists work in a huge variety of settings. This might include hospitals, schools, prisons, industry, and voluntary and charitable organisations. Physiotherapists also visit clients and their carers at home.

Physiotherapists work with babies, young children, adolescents, adults and older people to help them overcome the effects of disability caused by physical illness, ageing or accident. The profession offers enormous opportunities for career development and endless variety.

What do you want from your career?

By now you will have considered the factors that you feel will be important in your future career. Are you looking for opportunities to help people make positive changes, to enable people to improve their movement and function and take responsibility for their own health? Are you interested in researching and developing new treatments or strategies to promote improved health? Does the thought of teaching and helping others to learn inspire you? Do you wish to be a leader? If so, then physiotherapy will certainly fulfil these needs. If you are looking for a job as a carer, doing things for people and offering sympathy, then you are probably going to find physiotherapy is not the job for you.

Physiotherapists use their unique skills to understand an individual's specific functioning needs and seek to improve the physical problems exhibited throughout the body. They work with people of all ages in many different situations who may have neuromuscular, cardiovascular, respiratory or musculoskeletal problems.

If you were thinking that physiotherapists might not be involved in some of the things nurses do – like taking people to the toilet and other intimate tasks – then this is quite wrong. You may need to be involved in areas of people's lives that are very personal, when a person may be vulnerable. For example, you may be involved in discussing continence issues or you might need to advise on matters relating to intimacy. As a physiotherapist you may need to observe how a patient moves or you may need to manipulate a certain part of the body. This may require a patient to remove clothing. You should be prepared to face any topic your client feels is important to them and be able to work in some testing situations. It is therefore essential that you are professional at all times and can maintain confidentiality.

Case study: What physiotherapy is not – Siobhan Kelly

I am quite a sporty person and have always had a strong interest in anything to do with sport. So when applying to the BSc Physiotherapy course at my university I had the expectation that it was going to involve a lot of work and communication with sporting people and sports teams. However, I was pleasantly surprised that you learn about a wide range of health conditions and various aspects of healthcare in physiotherapy. It provides you with a vast range of skills and qualities that contribute to you as a person, who may be aspiring to gain employment within the healthcare system. Sports injuries and issues involving sports teams only make up a small percentage of the learning materials for the course. You get the opportunity to learn about breathing conditions, joint problems, pain, problems children may have, conditions associated with the brain and how the body works – the list is endless! When you actually put the information you have learned into practice you are able to see what a difference a physiotherapist can make to someone's life.

Can someone with a disability be a physiotherapist?

The Health and Care Professions Council (HCPC) is a regulatory body set up to maintain a register of health and care professionals who meet the required standards for safe and professional practice.

As long as you can meet the health requirements to register with the HCPC there should be no reason why you could not undertake the training to become a physiotherapist. Universities have support in place for people with specific learning needs. There are physiotherapists in practice who are visually impaired or who are deaf; some physiotherapists have dyslexia and some have mental health conditions.

What are the qualities of a good physiotherapist?

Physiotherapists need a range of skills, some of which you may already have and some of which you can learn. The skills can be divided into personal skills, practical skills and academic skills (see Figure 2.1).

It is important to develop all of these skills equally – it will not be possible to 'get by' with great academic skills if you find it very difficult to communicate with others or find it hard to carry out practical tasks.

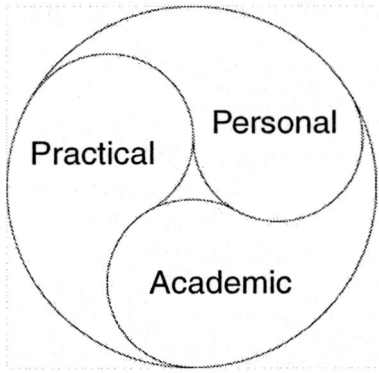

Figure 2.1: The range of physiotherapy skills

Personal skills

You will need to be a patient person, able to sit back and allow someone to tackle an activity at their own pace. If you get frustrated easily or feel you always need to be in control then you might find physiotherapy a frustrating career. Energy, resilience, determination and open mindedness are also essential. You will need excellent communication skills – written, verbal and non-verbal – and you should feel comfortable in the company of people of all ages, sexes, races and cultures. There is no room for discrimination in this career. You will need to demonstrate respectful and dignity-focused actions, and to be calm, confident and assertive. You will need these personal values and skills and will be able to advance them during your training.

Academic skills

These include literacy and numeracy skills, as all programmes will require you to have at least a GCSE (or equivalent) pass in both English Language and Mathematics. You may also need to have a science GCSE and should check with the universities which you are interested in to ensure you meet their criteria. Each university will also ask for A level (or equivalent) qualifications for those applying for a BSc programme and you will need to check each university for their requirements. All of the courses are listed on the Chartered Society of Physiotherapy website and specific information can be found on the university website or in their prospectus.

You will also need to be able to think critically about a subject. This means being able to assess information from all angles and feeling confident in drawing conclusions from your thoughts. The academic skills you will learn during your training are research skills, searching for information, referencing, reflecting and analysing.

Practical skills

Physiotherapy involves the application of physical interventions, which will require you to be able to adapt and problem-solve to meet individual needs. You will require co-ordination and dexterity but you do not need to be 'sporty'. You may be involved in exercise and movement, manual therapy or other treatment modalities but your skill base will develop with experience. You will also develop skills in moving and handling or first aid.

What relevant experience should I get?

It would be sensible to try to arrange an opportunity to shadow a physiotherapist before you apply to join a training programme. Many students say that they have come across physiotherapy due to either having experienced physiotherapy themselves or having observed the work of a physiotherapist with a relative or friend. This is very useful; however, it will only give a narrow view on this complex profession, so it is advisable to seek out other opportunities to see physiotherapy in action. As well as this, there are some very helpful resources on the Chartered Society of Physiotherapy website, with service users, carers and physiotherapists describing the work and its impact on people's lives.

All universities offer a range of discovery days and open days to enable you to decide which programme to choose. Admissions tutors are happy to help you with information and there is usually an opportunity to meet with students who are already undertaking the programme. Lots of the physiotherapy training programmes have Facebook pages where you can communicate with staff and students to get a feel for the programme and profession.

If you find it difficult to get a work placement or shadowing experience then giving some time to volunteer at a care home, for a youth group, as a Scout or Guide leader, at a school, day centre or with a charity will certainly give you an insight into working with a wide variety of people.

Working in a team

There will hardly ever be a situation when a physiotherapist is not working as part of a team. While you are at university there will be plenty of opportunities to develop your team-working skills as you undertake projects and research together. There will be groups and societies to join and many physiotherapy programmes have a physiotherapy society. You can also join a National or Regional Network and get involved with promoting physiotherapy, learning events and trade union activities. Being part of the professional community as a student member is time well spent, as it helps you to network with professionals and gives you access to a whole range of learning resources via the Chartered Society of Physiotherapy.

Assess your skills

Some team skills you will need are shown in Table 2.1. Which of these do you already have and which do you need to develop?

Listening	Negotiation	Reliability	Honesty
Trustworthiness	Communication	Understanding	Patience
Selflessness	Motivation	Assertiveness	Humility
Supportive	Responsive	Approachable	Collaboration

Table 2.1: Team skills for physiotherapy

Teams in practice will include a wide range of other professionals, volunteers, carers, families and of course your service users. Learning to work together and understand each other's roles is very important. This is referred to as 'inter-professional working' and physiotherapists tend to find that they have been well equipped to work like this because of the nature of their profession and the inter-professional training they have received (McKenna and Wright, 2012).

After you have qualified and had some experience working in practice, you might choose to apply for a team leader role. This could be within a physiotherapy team or an inter-professional team.

Top tip

You will need to demonstrate your team-working competency in your UCAS personal statement. There are several ways you could do this; for example, if you have had experience working in a team before in either a paid or voluntary capacity, if you have been an active member of a sports team, if you have been a young leader in Scouts or Guides and have earned your scout belt, if you have been part of a church group or if you have undertaken your Duke of Edinburgh's award. Reflect on your experiences and try to show how you have used them to develop your skills.

Understanding and communicating with people

As a physiotherapist you will be communicating with a wide range of people on a day to day basis. Physiotherapists work in a very wide range of services with people of all ages and cultures. You will need to have (or will need to develop) a range of communication styles, so that you feel confident and competent speaking in any given situation. During your training you will be given the opportunity to develop your verbal communication skills by taking part in presentations, mock interviews, debates, ward rounds and team meetings and you may have the opportunity to attend conflict resolution training. You will work with different students, lecturers and practice staff and learn when to switch from a formal style of communication to informal, as well as developing a style that is business-focused and a style that is person-focused.

During your training you will also develop your written communication skills. It is important that physiotherapists can write up their patient contact notes, write formal letters, and compose reports, service improvement plans and business cases. Writing up contemporaneous notes is a fundamental essential, so you will be given opportunities to develop this skill.

2: How do I know that physiotherapy is the right career for me?

Case study: Developing my skills – Emma St. John Hollis

The BSc (Hons) Physiotherapy Programme enables you to develop a number of key skills that will help to make you a well-rounded physiotherapist. Communication is important not only in the profession but also in everyday life. The course has helped me to develop my communication skills from talking to students and tutors to speaking to patients with dementia on placement. Being a course representative on the programme has improved my listening skills as I will collect feedback from the cohort and liaise with tutors. I would definitely recommend considering going for a course representative position as it helps to build on team and leadership skills as well as boosting your CV! The academic support from tutors through lectures, seminars, practical lab sessions and feedback enables you to fine tune the best learning methods for you as an individual by realising if you learn best practically, visually or through reading. Tutors also help to give advice on time management which is essential when you're trying to balance work and play whilst at university and in the working world. My therapeutic skills have also developed through a further understanding of anatomy and palpation and testing methods. The practice placements on the course give you a true insight into what it is like as a working physiotherapist. Seeing a variety of service users with a range of conditions helps you to develop your assessment and analytical skills whilst collaborating with the members of staff and family members of the patient. The course has enabled many to become confident and competent physiotherapy graduates that can work in a variety of environments and areas of the profession.

Two of the skills you will need to develop are active listening and observation. Physiotherapists spend time listening to their clients; after all, the client's views on their condition will help the physiotherapist to formulate the optimum treatment plan. Physiotherapists also watch how their clients undertake practical activities and assess behaviours.

Assess your skills

- Listen to a friend talking about something they have been doing. Afterwards, write down as much as you can remember – all the little details – and then ask your friend to check to see if you remembered correctly.

- Watch how someone walks upstairs. Can you spot all the different movements they make? Do they do this in the same way that you would? What is different?

You will need to assess your own non-verbal communication too. It is important that your actions match your words and that your face does not send a message to a client that might be misunderstood. For example, if you walked into a house that was dirty and had an unpleasant aroma, would you be able to carry on without screwing up your face? It is easy to lose your client's trust if they see you reacting negatively.

Chapter summary

Many students have a personal reason for wanting to become a physiotherapist. As physiotherapy can be many things to many people, the key to successful study is an open mind and the ability to see things from as many viewpoints as possible. Once you have assessed your personal skills you will have a baseline for the start of your study. You can be sure that, with so many interesting topics to cover, your training programme will fly by and you will be eagerly preparing for your first post.

Chapters 11 and 12 provide a range of examples of the work physiotherapists might be involved in and provide a good starting point for understanding the role of physiotherapists.

Key points

- Try to meet up with or shadow physiotherapists in both physical and mental health roles.
- Physiotherapists need a mixture of academic, personal and practical skills.
- You will need team-working skills and excellent observation and listening skills.
- You will need patience and to be able to sit back as people try to develop their independence.
- Your non-verbal communication needs to match your verbal communication.

Useful resources

The Chartered Society of Physiotherapy: www.csp.org.uk

References

Chartered Society of Physiotherapy (2013) *What is physiotherapy?* [Online]. Available from: www.csp.org.uk/your-health/what-physiotherapy [Accessed 31 January 2017].

McKenna, C. and Wright, C. (2012) Occupational Therapists. In: Littlechild, B. and Smith, R. (eds.) (2012) *A Handbook for Inter-professional Practice in Human Services: Learning to Work Together.* Edinburgh, Pearson. pp. 249–259.

Chapter 3

How do I choose which course and university to apply to?

Deciding how and where you should study can be a very difficult decision to make and will involve people other than yourself. Take the time to discuss this with others. Parents, guardians, partners, spouses and children all have a significant voice which should be considered in the decision-making process as they are going to be affected. Teachers and admissions tutors will have experience and perspectives which they will be happy to share with you. In all cases they wish you to have the best experience and the best opportunities. There are also many support websites and books which will provide you with information on physiotherapy. Tap into this knowledge and make your judgements based on the best available information. Organisations such as the Chartered Society of Physiotherapy and the Health and Care Professions Council have literature and web pages dedicated to the interested student. As you consider individual programmes and universities, explore their prospectuses and websites to ensure that you are fully informed regarding what they offer.

This chapter provides you with advice on what to look for as you explore the available information. It will also help you to determine what is important to you in the decision-making process. As you review each section try to note what your preference is for each issue, as this will help you to focus your thinking. Please note that references to universities in this book will focus purely on the physiotherapy programmes and the information given should not be assumed for any other programmes delivered at that institution.

Location – does it matter?

We are all different. While some have a preference to live close to family and friends, others prefer to experience living far away. The locations of universities fall into different categories. There are those which are based in a city centre campus; others are out of town. In some, physiotherapy is taught in the same location as the rest of the student body; in others physiotherapy students are taught separately from the rest of the university. This section explores these differences and considers the advantages and limitations of each.

Some universities are based further out of town like Plymouth University or Northumbria University Newcastle and offer a range of opportunities. Things are usually quieter both on and off campus and this will suit those who prefer fewer distractions than being in a city centre. Access to facilities may be limited to those provided by the university and to access community facilities it may be that you require a car or will need to make use of local public transport and taxi services in order to fully experience student life.

Many universities, such as Leeds Beckett, Coventry and Teesside Universities, are located close to the city centre. These universities are situated next to the main shopping thoroughfares and are also very close to main train and bus stations. For you as a student, this can be a life saver (or at least a money saver). Being close to the town means that you have access to all the facilities you need without having to travel far. The cost of living will be greatly reduced as taxis or bus fares may not be required and you may be able to walk home from nights out. Being close to social and shopping spaces also helps you to keep busy and means there is always something to do away from the university. However, there may be some disadvantages. For example, accommodation may be older and may be adapted rather than purpose built. That being said, universities have done much to counteract these problems and provide excellent accommodation for students.

> 'I was determined to study in a city as I had lived in a remote village. I wanted to challenge myself and moving to Manchester certainly did that. I hoped to see a different side to life and the placements I went on enabled me to consider issues I had never come across before. It helped me grow and I liked it so much I stayed there after I qualified.'

Occasionally, universities have expanded beyond their original campus to use alternative sites. This could mean the physiotherapy programme is delivered off the main campus. It may also mean students are separated from the main student facilities including the library. While this separation may suit some students, making them feel exceptional, it may make others feel isolated from the rest of the student body. This is a rare situation, as most programmes will be delivered on a campus with the rest of the students and accessible onsite facilities; however, it is worth considering such a scenario when thinking about where to apply.

Where the course is based should be considered when choosing where to study. If you have already been to university you may be less interested in what is on campus or what social life is available. Certain towns and cities might be more appealing and the actual campus less relevant. These issues should be considered when deciding where to study.

> **Top tip**
>
> When you go to look at the university, have a look at the town or city too. If you can stay overnight you will get a feel for the location at different times of day and this might help you to make your final decision.

Should I live at home?

This may not be a concern for some students. For many the decision regarding where to study is dictated by finance, family commitment and convenience. For those seeking a new life and adventure then this might not even be a topic for discussion. If you are unsure you may wish to consider the following points.

Leaving home can be a difficult decision. It demands that you begin to fend for yourself. You will have all the freedom you have ever wanted. No one will tell you what to do, there are no parental rules, you can eat what you want and get up when you like. As in all situations in life there are obligations and responsibilities associated with these rights. You have to look after yourself: this means doing your own cooking, your own laundry and your own cleaning up. Occasionally you might even consider doing your own ironing. You also have to take responsibility for your own bills – rent, TV, internet, Council Tax, water, electricity and gas. The accommodation you choose may include some of these elements, but the costs will still need to be met. Being away from home also means you may feel homesick. Many students experience this to some extent and it will lessen over time, but it can be distracting from your studies.

Living at home can also bring its own difficulties. As you are developing your skills as an adult and trying to maintain a degree of independence, this can be challenged by a well-meaning family. As you are trying to learn, the demands of the family may distract you from your studies. This can be particularly difficult when you are working on assignments or trying to meet submission deadlines. It can also be difficult bringing home new university friends. If you are commuting some distance it may be hard for you to mix with the other students on your course who are in halls together or able to socialise together more easily.

Ultimately this decision will be based on who you are, your commitments and what you want from the experience. Only you can decide what you have at home and what the university can offer you.

What courses are available?

The Chartered Society of Physiotherapy (CSP) website contains a complete list of all courses approved by the CSP in the UK. It shows a great number of different programmes across the country. These have been developed, in the main, as variations of the standard undergraduate programme. Information can also be found on the appropriate UCAS websites.

The three-year BSc (Honours) route is the standard programme across England and Wales. In Scotland this route is a four-year programme. This route normally runs full time from September and will accommodate the majority of A level or equivalent applicants but will also accept students who may have already completed a degree previously.

Accelerated postgraduate programmes have become popular over the past few years. These routes run full time over a period of two years. They cater for applicants who have already completed a degree in another subject but wish to train as a physiotherapist. For most of these programmes there is an expectation that applicants hold a degree in a related subject or that they have some experience working in health or social care. On successful completion of the programme graduates are awarded a Postgraduate Diploma in Physiotherapy or an MSc in Physiotherapy. Both of these awards will normally be accepted by the Health and Care Professions Council for registration purposes.

The in-service BSc Honours degree and part-time BSc Honours degree are part-time programmes which have been developed for staff currently working in a support role within health or social care. They undertake the programme with the support of their employer. Attendance is normally part time and the student continues in their employed role for the remainder of the week.

There are a number of part-time BSc Honours degree programmes which are similar to the in-service routes but it is not necessary for the applicant to be working in health or social care. When considering the part-time route it is important to clarify the entry requirements. Students can also undertake a full-time work-based learning BSc Honours degree. This takes two and a half years to complete.

At the time of going to press there are initiatives to offer apprenticeships in physiotherapy. Whilst there is very limited information about this at present, the Chartered Society of Physiotherapy website will be the best place to follow the progress of their development.

In the long term you must apply for whichever programme is best for you. There may be no choice for some people, while others may have a number of options. Although you may already work in healthcare it may not be convenient to undertake a part-time programme. You may prefer to leave work and focus full time on your studies. Although you may already have a degree it might not be appropriate for you to undertake the postgraduate route and therefore you could apply to an undergraduate programme for your study. In making the decision it is worth reflecting on your reason for undertaking the programme: are you motivated more by the achievement of a qualification or by the training you will undertake to become a physiotherapist? This may serve as the final factor in the decision-making process.

Postgraduate or undergraduate?

This may be a dilemma for a number of students who already hold an undergraduate qualification. There are over a dozen programmes across the UK, from Eastbourne to Edinburgh, offering postgraduate opportunities. These have been designed to provide an accelerated route through the required training in order that an individual can more quickly practise as a qualified and registered physiotherapist. These courses have all been accredited or approved by the Chartered Society of Physiotherapy and the Health and Care Professions Council and meet the rigorous standards required of these organisations. However, this route may not meet the needs of everyone.

Due to the nature of these programmes the traditional student vacations may be reduced in order to create additional study time in the two years to achieve all the required objectives. This would result in students having only short periods out of study where they might reflect and re-energise.

This route might also be particularly challenging where a student takes time to settle in a new context. By their nature these programmes assume prior study skills and will encourage the student to draw upon them. There will be little by way of induction to university skills and you will be expected to begin the programme ready to learn. A significant prior knowledge of relevant anatomy and physiology is expected by most institutions offering a postgraduate physiotherapy programme. While you will not be expected to have prior knowledge regarding physiotherapy theory and practice, there will be an assumption that you will quickly and earnestly engage in self-directed study to develop that understanding. Teaching strategies have been developed to support a more mature approach to learning. More autonomy will be expected and there will be an assumption that you will have greater motivation and self-discipline.

With these expectations you may feel it would be more appropriate that you undertake the undergraduate route to physiotherapy. This will not diminish your employment opportunities but will give you more time to process the new learning and make sense of the information you are required to handle. This may be particularly true for those graduates who are entering physiotherapy from an unrelated field. While you will bring many transferable skills to a postgraduate programme, there may be a lot of new information which needs to be understood while being able to work academically at Master's rather than undergraduate level.

Ultimately this comes down to a personal decision. You know what your work capabilities are and what you might be able to achieve. You may have plans for the future that require an accelerated training. You may have children or other family commitments which would be more problematic in either of the routes available. Only you can determine the course you wish to pursue. If you have any doubts discuss this with the admissions tutors, listen to their advice and then draw your own conclusion.

Case study: A BSc (Honours) programme – Sophie Warnes

I am currently in my first year of a Physiotherapy degree course at university. At the moment I am nearing the end of my first term which has been very intense, yet very interesting and I've loved every minute. We have covered anatomy and physiology in the programme, including practical work and placement. I have thoroughly enjoyed placement so far at a local hospital physiotherapy department. I was very passionate about observing the rehabilitation of knee and hip replacements and also respiratory exercises. This gives us a good insight into the job role, and how qualified physiotherapists deal with different situations. Being at university and on placement as a whole has given me a much wider understanding of the role and the effects it can have on people in the community. This job seems to be very rewarding, especially to help people in pain and give them some relief even though this can sometimes be temporary. On the whole, I am finding the degree a very enlightening experience and I am sure it will be a great benefit to me in the future. Although it's very intense with exams and revision, I always look forward to reaping the rewards of all the hard work it involves and strive to be a very valued member of society in the future.

Should I worry about reputation?

Every year there are a variety of league tables published which indicate that one university is better than another. The problem with league tables is that they do not always measure the things which you as a student are interested in, nor do they give a true picture of the course you are intending to study. The difficulty that you have, therefore, is determining from this information what is important to you. Certainly, a review of some of the major newspapers will highlight some significant and rigorous data. These league tables consider issues such as staff:student ratios, teaching quality, quality of research and entry tariff points, but they represent the whole university and not necessarily the programme you are about to undertake. In 2016 in one national newspaper university league table, of the universities listed, only 2 of the top 20 had a physiotherapy programme and there were only 6 in the top 50. Yet these 6 programmes deliver extremely high-quality training. The things which they do well may simply not be measured in the columns of the league tables. These might include student support, attrition rates or development of communication and management skills, attributes which may never be shown in a league table. It is important to understand that every programme meets the approval standards of the Health and Care Professions Council and has received approval from the Chartered Society of Physiotherapy as well as international recognition.

So if you are to ignore the league tables how do you determine where to go? What may be of more value is the National Student Survey (NSS). This is an annual survey taken by the final year students of all undergraduate programmes in the UK. The survey reports on the student experience of each programme. This is not without difficulties. Different subjects are grouped together into categories and physiotherapy normally appears in 'Anatomy, Physiology and Pathology'. Depending on the university, it may be the only subject in this category or it may be one of several subjects. Despite this, the results can provide some indication of the student experience. The NSS gives final year undergraduates the opportunity to provide feedback on their courses in a nationally recognised format. Students on flexible courses will be asked to participate as they near the end of their course but not necessarily in their final year. There are 23 core questions, relating to a variety of aspects of the student learning experience:

- Teaching on the course
- Assessment and feedback
- Academic support
- Organisation and management
- Learning resources

- Personal development
- Overall satisfaction
- Students' union

This data is also available with the opportunity for comparison, through the Unistats web pages. The address can be found at the end of this chapter.

Students are also given the opportunity to provide comments on their experience as a whole. While this information is forwarded to the university to help them identify how they can make improvements, it is not available to the public.

If you are considering applying to undertake a postgraduate course, the Postgraduate Taught Experience Survey will give you an idea of how postgraduate students viewed their learning experience. The results of the survey are available on the Higher Education Academy website. Postgraduate programmes are normally delivered by the same team as the undergraduate route and therefore much of the NSS data will also be reflective of all routes being delivered. Ultimately, your choice of programme should not be based on league tables or opinions, but on your own view of what you see and experience. If you can, go to the campus and look around. If you can meet staff, do so and get a feel for the department. When you are being interviewed remember that you are deciding if this is a suitable place for you to study. After all, you will be spending several years of your life there; if you feel uncomfortable, then it will be a very difficult experience. Make sure that the programme is delivered in a way which best meets your learning style. We will cover issues about learning styles later in this chapter.

What is the course structure?

There are a variety of different types of programme extending from two to four years. It is not practical to explore each of these individually but there are some key elements which will be found across all programmes and some things you may need to consider. These elements should be explored when considering a programme and taken into account when finally making your decision.

The starting dates of programmes differ. While most routes will commence in the autumn, there are some programmes which start in January, February and April. This may have a bearing on your studies and preparation to undertake the programme. This will also have an impact on when you will complete the course and when you will be available to work. It may be an advantage to be looking for work at a time when the majority of final year students are still completing their studies.

All programmes approved by the Chartered Society of Physiotherapy require students to successfully complete a minimum of 1,000 hours of practice placements. This gives students the opportunity to work with service users in real work situations while being supported by experienced physiotherapists. The placements will be organised in a variety of health and social care environments providing a range of learning opportunities. These placements will be interspersed throughout the programme. These placements break up the time spent in the university and offer you the opportunity to apply the theory you have learned in the practice context. Chapter 8 will provide more detailed information on this aspect of your training. Occasionally some programmes teach across the traditional university vacation periods. This may mean that summer breaks are shorter or placements take you into winter or spring holiday periods.

On modular programmes you may be studying a number of modules simultaneously with assessments spread across the year or perhaps all the assessments focused into a key week or fortnight. Whichever method is used, these modules will have been organised in this way to offer the best learning experience and will have taken account of feedback from staff and students.

How do they teach and how do I learn?

For many years academics and researchers have debated the best way to teach students. While this has now tended towards the concept of lecture followed by seminar and then a tutorial, there is still much variation within and beyond this combination. As with other aspects of deciding on a university, considering which teaching methods suit you best is a matter of personal preference. The common practice is for all teaching to be divided into modules. Each module will identify and deliver certain learning outcomes which will be assessed. Modules will be of varying sizes and contain a variety of assessments proportionate to their size. Sometimes these modules may be very small 10-credit modules. Other modules are much larger representing perhaps 60 credits or more. These credits represent the number of hours spent studying a particular topic so a 60-credit module will therefore require 6 times more study time than a 10-credit module. This might be linked to a final dissertation or major project. A 10-credit module may represent 100 hours of study, but perhaps only 20 hours of this will take place in a classroom. You will be expected to complete 80 hours through self-directed study.

Some programmes will deliver the module in very short periods, for example as a block of full-time study on a single module over a week. On the plus side, this ensures you work on the material but it also means that you do not have time to reflect on your learning. Other programmes might deliver a module for two hours each week throughout the whole academic year. While this offers lots of opportunity to read and reflect on your learning, it is limited by a lack of focus and emphasis in what may be a very busy week. Your own approach to learning might fit well with either of these or a version somewhere in between.

The other main strategy which is employed in teaching physiotherapy students is problem-based learning (PBL). This teaching strategy is not new, having been developed in Canada in the 1960s. PBL requires students to work together in groups of about eight to resolve often complex problems. These are given in a variety of forms, including paper case studies, visual, written or audio material. Students acquire subject knowledge and skills through the resolution of these problems which may have a professional context rather than working with the primary knowledge base in isolation. Teaching staff will serve as facilitators rather than tutors or lecturers, leaving students to manage the depth and breadth of learning based on their own experience, needs and expectations. Depending on the programme, PBL may be used as the basis for structuring the whole curriculum, or may be seen as a means of introducing problem-solving exercises into a traditional curriculum.

Top tip

When you attend open days remember to ask the staff and students about the teaching styles that are used, so that you can assess whether they match your preferred learning style.

How will I be assessed?

Assessment comes in a variety of forms and each assessment on your programme will have been designed to give you the best opportunity to learn. Assessment will allow you to develop skills in preparation for your future role as a physiotherapist. It also serves to test your understanding of material and provide an objective evaluation of your progression.

While you may be familiar with or expect formal examinations, these are likely to comprise only a small part of the assessment process. A variety of different assessment methods will be employed as this mix allows individual strengths to be exhibited and will make demands on a range of skills. In many cases you will be assessed in a traditional written essay format. Assessments might also include case study work, group work, presentations and the production of posters. Occasionally, there may be assessed tutorials or oral examinations. Practical skills will invariably be assessed through demonstration with practical exams used to assess academic, university based modules. Practice placements are another example of this kind of assessment, where the placement educator will assess how, for example, you carry out your treatment plans. When considering a programme of study it would be useful to enquire about the types of assessment used and consider if this suits your own learning and assessment style.

Assessment can be one of two types: summative or formative. Summative assessments are those for which you will receive a mark or grade and which will contribute to your progression and final degree classification. Formative assessment is used to inform you of your progression. You will receive feedback on all of your assessments either as a grade or as written feedback which indicates the strengths and limitations of your submitted work. Often you will receive both types of feedback. When you receive this feedback it is being provided in order that you might improve your skills and understanding. Whether you have been successful or otherwise, this feedback will assist your subsequent work. It is a reflection of your work and not you and should be reviewed to inform future submissions.

Case study: Studying with dyslexia – Simon Little

As a student with dyslexia it can be a daunting prospect when beginning studying and the best piece of advice I can offer is to embrace the services and facilities which are available. Support can come through both the university and course funding body in the form of a disabled student allowance. The latter is a fund that students can use towards assistive technology, which has greatly aided me with my studies. I personally find that using a computer to make notes and reviewing them before commencing lectures allows me time to comprehend theory and ask questions if required. Also, I find that having the opportunity to audio record lectures makes revision more manageable as I can review notes and listen to the lecture multiple times. I have had a positive experience through my studies with all academic staff being extremely accommodating to my learning needs. However, being honest and openly discussing my individual learning style with academic tutors and practice placement educators as early as possible meant that my learning requirements could be factored into potential learning opportunities. Disclosing your individual needs will ensure a positive learning experience and helps academic staff in understanding how best to assist where necessary. Embrace all of the support available, yet be proactive and find the best approach for you.

Becoming a Physiotherapist

Chapter summary

Whether you plan to live at home or move away, there are many aspects to take into consideration before selecting where to apply. Taking the time to study your options will help to reduce the number of surprises later, so if you really don't enjoy exams then it is wise to look closely at the assessment methods in each programme!

Assessing your academic ability in order to select the correct level of study is important too. Even if you already have a degree, you should consider both the BSc and the MSc programmes and seek the advice of the admissions tutors. Ensure you seek out learning support before starting the programme so that you can have any requirements in place.

Key points

- Check the UCAS and Chartered Society of Physiotherapy websites for all the available courses – choose the level of study that is best for you.
- Look at the National Student Survey and the Postgraduate Taught Experience Survey results.
- Consider the practicalities – where you will live and how far you can realistically travel.
- Check the course structure – does it suit your learning style and personal commitments?

Useful resources

Chartered Society of Physiotherapy: www.csp.org.uk

Higher Education Academy Postgraduate Taught Experience Survey: www.heacademy.ac.uk/research/surveys/postgraduate-taught-experience-survey-ptes

NSS results: http://unistats.direct.gov.uk

Chapter 4

How do I apply?

BPP
UNIVERSITY
SCHOOL OF HEALTH

In this chapter we consider all of the elements of the application process. For most applicants, physiotherapy is their dream profession and they will be extremely motivated to prepare their application form well.

The number of places on physiotherapy programmes differs at each university and that competition for those places is fierce. You should take time to look at all the available programmes (you can find this information on the Chartered Society of Physiotherapy website) to ensure you are applying for the courses that suit you best. It is sensible to contact admissions tutors to ask about the programme and whether it is possible to attend a discovery or open day as this should help you to decide which programmes to apply for.

All physiotherapy programmes require you to have a Disclosure and Barring Service (DBS) check. This will usually be an enhanced check as you will be working with children and vulnerable people. If you think that you might have something on a DBS that may preclude you from undertaking the programme you may wish to check this out with the admissions tutor before you send in your application. On an enhanced check any caution or conviction is listed, even those considered a minor. Physiotherapy programmes do have the responsibility of checking this as it would be irresponsible to train you only to find that something from your past prevented you from being able to register with the Health and Care Professions Council (the regulatory body with whom all physiotherapists must register in order to work as a physiotherapist).

The Universities and Colleges Admission System (UCAS)

Using the UCAS system online is the usual way to apply for Bachelor of Science with Honours (BSc (Hons)) programmes in the UK. The UCAS website has easy to follow steps with plenty of useful tips to help you through the process. You can apply for up to six programmes. The number of programmes you can apply for depends on the fee you pay. It is important that you get your application in on time, correctly completed and then track your progress using UCAS Track. It is useful to note that many universities are now using the 'gathered field' system, which means that they are waiting until all the interviews have been undertaken before offering any places. This might mean that you could wait for some considerable time before finding out if you have been successful in your application. You may wish to check with admissions tutors to see which method they are following. If you are not successful in your first applications then you may be able to apply through the UCAS Extra system or through the UCAS clearing system, which begins after 30 June. If you are offered the opportunity to use UCAS Extra take the time to review your personal statement. This is because it is likely that whatever is written there has not met the criteria that admissions tutors are looking for.

Direct application

For Master of Science (MSc) programmes you will generally need to make a direct application to the university of your choice. You should be able to access and download the application forms online from the individual university websites but, if not, just ring the admissions team to request that the forms are sent to you. Some universities will only have a small number of available places and may interview you and keep you on a waiting list if the places are full until the next academic year.

What do the admissions team look for?

Remember that not all universities are the same – some will interview you for a place and others will make their decision from your application form. You may wish to consider contacting the admissions tutor to arrange to meet with them or to chat over the phone, to get an idea of the criteria they will be using. You should refer to the information that you will find in the university prospectus and website as well as the course information that you can find on the Chartered Society of Physiotherapy website. Additionally, you may know someone who is already on the programme or you could contact current students on their Facebook page. Ask around and see what you can find out about the programme you want to undertake. One thing admissions tutors are definitely looking for is a form that has been completed correctly!

Your form may be initially reviewed by a member of administration staff who is filtering all of the applications. This person will be checking to see that you have the correct qualifications. If you are applying from outside of the UK then it is wise to check that you have the correct qualifications before applying. A quick phone call or email to the admissions office at the university should clarify this for you.

Your personal statement

If everyone who applies has the required UCAS points and has completed the form correctly then how do admissions tutors and teams make any decisions? The best opportunity for you to demonstrate your commitment to your study and chosen profession is on the personal statement – so make sure it is something you take time to prepare. It is an opportunity to demonstrate that you are well informed about the profession and the university you are applying to.

It is important to explain how the skills you have will be useful and demonstrate how you have developed those skills. Try not to base the whole statement on a story of how, for example, a member of your family was treated by a physiotherapist and you thought it looked like a fulfilling career. If you have seen a physiotherapist at work, demonstrate your understanding of what you have seen. Explain if you have been able to undertake some work experience and what you were able to learn from this. If you have attended a discovery day or an open day, give an example of how this helped to confirm that physiotherapy was the career for you. Remember to cover aspects like teamwork, communication and leadership. Try to help the admissions tutor imagine you on their programme.

If you are applying for an MSc programme the admissions tutors are likely to be seeking evidence that you understand how your first degree, and your personal experiences of academic study, have prepared you for Master's level study. If you show that you recognise the difference between undergraduate and Master's level study in your personal statement this may begin to help you to demonstrate your suitability for the programme.

Case study: The admissions process – Tom Kirwan

The admissions process, what can I say? As with any interview you'll ever do in your life, it is not going to be easy and in hindsight, it was the hardest interview I have ever had to endure. The physiotherapy degree is one of the most over-subscribed courses in the UK; it is not designed to be 'easy'. The interview process I undertook was essentially split into two; I sat in a group interview with fellow applicants and we were given a topic to discuss. That was it. Simple. The real purpose of this is to assess and evaluate your ability and skills working within a team, because you are going to be working alongside other valued healthcare professionals throughout your career. It is an important quality to have. The second part of the interview was one to one and this was the opportunity to sell myself to the university. They want to know why they should choose you, rather than the hundreds of other applicants. It all sounds scary and formal but it is not. The assessors have been applicants before; they know exactly what it is like. Every minute you are there they are welcoming, encouraging and reassuring, because you might be the next best physiotherapist out there.

The interview process

Not all universities interview prospective physiotherapy students in a traditional way, so it is imperative that you make your personal statement as good as it can be, because you may or may not get a place purely on what is written there. For the universities that do interview prospective students you may find that you wait slightly longer to find out if you have been offered a conditional or unconditional place. The interviews come in two different forms – either an individual interview or an interview within a group – with no two universities doing the same thing. Some universities may conduct a traditional interview, some offer an interview plus some group activities and others just conduct group and individual activities, designed to find out about your skills in practice. You may find that physiotherapists from practice and service users are also involved in the process. Both of these will need prior preparation on your part.

Individual interviews

Some people really enjoy interviews as it gives them the opportunity to sell themselves and demonstrate verbally how they feel they will be successful. Remember that the people interviewing you are not trying to find out that you know all about physiotherapy and they are certainly not trying to trip you up or make you feel incompetent. They are trying to find out what makes you the person you are, what sort of values you have and whether you have an enquiring mind. They will be asking questions to see whether you think quickly and creatively and to find out how you view the world around you.

Group interviews

The size of the group you might be in will vary and there will usually be at least two staff members there. The purpose of a group interview is to see how you interact with your fellow interviewees – do you contribute to the discussion? Are you silent throughout? Do you take over and prevent others from speaking? Do you listen to what others are saying? Are you able to encourage other applicants to participate? Are you able to challenge in an assertive way or do you let others get their own way? Do you look interested in what is going on around you or does it look like you'd rather be somewhere else? You will need to be conscious of your non-verbal behaviours as well as your verbal contribution. Remember to be your own person; don't just follow the rest – especially if you have a different view.

4: How do I apply?

Top tips – Interview advice

- Plan your travel arrangements and try to arrive with time to spare.
- Wear something smart but comfortable.
- Avoid too much make up and jewellery and avoid fiddling with scarves.
- Take certificates and any other useful evidence of your achievements with you in an appropriate, tidy, clean file.
- Make sure you are sitting in a comfortable position – try not to fidget.
- Make good eye contact with the people who are interviewing you.
- Ask to have a question repeated if you don't understand it or need more time – no one is trying to trick you.
- Make sure you answer the question – give an example to help show your competence or understanding.
- Ask some sensible questions at the end of your interview.
- If you don't feel you have had the opportunity to tell the panel something significant about yourself then tell them at the end.
- Leave the panel with a really positive image of you.
- **Smile!**

Group activities

Some programmes may ask you to participate in other activities at your interview. These could be team tasks or even demonstrating how you would make a concise summary of a series of paragraphs from a book or an article. The reason for undertaking these tasks is to give you an opportunity to demonstrate how you work within a team or to show how you are able to read and understand the important points from a passage in a short period of time.

There are many practical skills which a prospective physiotherapy student would benefit from having – these are sometimes difficult to convey on an application form, therefore the admissions team is offering you the chance to demonstrate them – so try not to get too anxious. Again, no one is trying to catch you out; try to relax and do your best.

It is important for you to know that in devising the application and interview process, many universities have consulted service users and carers, as well as employers, to see what sort of characteristics they all feel are important for physiotherapy students to have. This isn't just about academic ability – you need to be an all-rounder. So if service users and carers have said that it is important for physiotherapists to demonstrate good listening skills it will be important for you to demonstrate this in your interview or activity. Employers may say that assertiveness is a key skill – so you'll need to show that too. Try to imagine the skills and personal attributes that you would value in a healthcare professional working with you, then assess if you can demonstrate those skills in your interview.

Case study: Service users' involvement in the admissions process – Janet Walker

One of my first roles at the university as a service user was that of assisting in interviewing candidates for places on the BSc programmes. The thing I found most interesting about being involved in the interview process was the way in which it was structured. Candidates were assessed in different ways, taking part in a group discussion as well as having formal discussions with the academic and clinical staff. It was interesting to observe different attitudes and responses from the candidates. I felt the interview process was less formal and less intimidating than individual interviews would have been on their own. In deciding who to offer places to it was interesting to listen to the other interviewers' views and opinions. I was made to feel that my opinions mattered and felt valued and part of a team.

Feedback

If you have attended an interview and are not fortunate enough to be offered a place, it is important to contact the university and ask if it would be possible to have some feedback about your performance. This might feel uncomfortable at first, but it is a valuable way to find out how well you did and to get some information to help improve your performance in future. When you make the telephone call, ensure you have paper and a pen to hand so you can jot down the constructive feedback that you should be given. Try not to be defensive about it – remember that other people may not see you as you see yourself. They are giving you honest feedback in the hope that it will be useful to you.

> 'When I wasn't successful at my first interview I contacted the university to ask for feedback. I was nervous and unsure what they would say, but the feedback I was given was very useful. I didn't realise that my eye contact had been at the floor rather than at the interview panel and that I had given very brief answers. The tutor advised me to give examples when I answered the questions too. I followed the feedback and felt more confident at my next interview, which must have come across to the panel as I was offered a place.'

You might choose to work on the feedback by yourself or you could consider taking the feedback to your careers adviser, personal tutor or a friend and work through the points with them. It might be helpful to undertake a practice interview to build up your skills too. This could be with a family member or a friend.

What if I still have questions?

It is good to have questions about the programme and there are several ways to find out the answers. General questions about physiotherapy can be answered by the student officer at the Chartered Society of Physiotherapy. You can contact them via the website. Specific questions about the individual physiotherapy programmes can be answered by the admissions tutor. These people are usually contactable by telephone or email, and you will be able to find their contact details on the university website. Don't be afraid to ask your question – if you need to know something then others may too, and it will help the universities when they review the information they provide for prospective students. You might want to follow physiotherapists on Facebook or Twitter. As well as the Chartered Society of Physiotherapy and the World Confederation for Physical Therapy you will be able to find many individual physiotherapists on social networking sites. You will also find the student physiotherapy groups for lots of universities, both in the UK and abroad. You can post questions and you'll find that students are happy to tell you the answers about their own university. You might want to know about how students formally evaluate physiotherapy programmes and you will find this out if you look at the National Student Survey and the Postgraduate Taught Experience Survey results.

So, hopefully you are now ready to start to prepare your application. Remember to leave sufficient time to research your chosen course and complete the forms, as your future career could depend on how thorough you are at this stage.

Becoming a Physiotherapist

It is important to demonstrate your enthusiasm and understanding of physiotherapy on your application form. You need to stand out from the rest of the applicants, so think widely about how to link your skills and experiences to show how you are the best applicant for the place. If you are offered an interview, follow the advice given earlier in this chapter, go with a positive outlook and be yourself.

4: How do I apply?

Chapter summary

It is important to demonstrate your enthusiasm and understanding of physiotherapy on your application form. You need to stand out from the rest of the applicants, so think widely about how to link your skills and experiences to show how you are the best applicant for the place. If you are offered an interview, follow the advice given earlier in this chapter, go with a positive outlook and be yourself.

Key points

- Check your DBS status – clarify the position with the Health and Care Professions Council if you are unsure.
- Attend discovery days or open days – and ask questions.
- Prepare your application forms – check for spelling and grammatical errors and ensure all the required information is completed.
- Arrange a practice interview with a friend – even if you don't need one, this is a useful thing to do.
- Prepare for your interview, read some up to date physiotherapy literature, visit a physiotherapist at work and find something smart but comfortable to wear (and polish your shoes!).
- Plan your travel arrangements so that you arrive safely and calmly for your interview.

Useful resources

Health and Care Professions Council: www.hcpc-uk.org

The Universities and Colleges Admissions Service: www.ucas.com

Results of the National Student Survey and Postgraduate Taught Experience Survey: http://unistats.direct.gov.uk

Chapter 5

What is life like as a student?

5: What is life like as a student?

Even if you have been a college or university student before, life as a physiotherapy student, studying for a professional qualification, is quite different. This chapter contains information to help you to plan for the years of study ahead.

Accommodation

Where you are going to live as a student is a very important decision and should not be taken without thorough consideration. Whatever you choose you will have to live with it for the next few months. There are a number of options available to you. Here we will consider the main ones.

Living in student halls

Student halls are a great way to begin your time at university. These are often managed by the university and will have all the basics required for life at university. There are sometimes opportunities to have all your meals included in this package. While being more expensive than other options, there is a degree of certainty in this accommodation and parents often value the additional assurance that this may provide. You will meet lots of new people who are studying a wide range of subjects. This helps you to mix with people other than physiotherapists. Sharing a building with lots of other people will also create some difficulties as not everyone wishes to study, sleep or respect the privacy of others as much as you do. While this is rarely a problem, some people will prefer to use halls only for their first year. This leaves some other considerations.

Living in a shared house

This might happen in one of two ways. The accommodation office at the university might indicate this as an option and you will be placed in a house with other students allocated to the same type of housing. This is similar in experience to student halls, but on a smaller scale. You are now self-catering and you don't have someone who comes in and cleans your room. The other approach to sharing a house often occurs during your later years of study. You get together with some friends and arrange to rent a house together, usually from a private landlord. This is often the cheapest way of living. You may be paying your own bills as well as your living costs, and this must be taken into account when you make your decision.

Renting a room

For those who are looking for a home away from home this is the choice for you. It is sometimes possible to rent a room in someone else's home. This will provide you with your own bedroom with study area and usually access to the kitchen. Occasionally you may have meals provided within the cost of the accommodation. This is often a great option as you are in someone else's home, with all the advantages of this. Bear in mind that they may not appreciate you coming in at 3:30am after socialising with your student friends and telling the whole house about it. It is, after all, their home. This type of accommodation may isolate you from the other students but may suit your personality.

There is no 'right' answer regarding which accommodation to choose. You must look for something that will be suitable for you. Contact the university accommodation office and they will be able to help you consider your options.

Finance

This will be considered in more detail in the next chapter. Being a student will usually require personal sacrifice and it will be necessary for you to adjust your finances in order to survive the budgetary restrictions which might be imposed by attending university. There is a culture of debt associated with being at university and while this is inevitable it should not be a burden nor should it be ignored. Read Chapter 6 for more information on how this might be managed.

Timetables

Your time at university is going to be managed through a timetable system. This will be very similar to the one in place at your college or school. You may be expected to attend sessions which are spread across a large campus or even on two different sites. It is not true that the timetable is constructed to make things as difficult as possible for students but it does have to fit in with the timetable of thousands of other students, staff and rooms! This will mean that occasionally a class will run during the evening or as early as 9:00am. This is a fact of life and it is your responsibility to be there. Attendance on many physiotherapy programmes is monitored and so it is important that you do attend or you may find yourself having to explain your absences to the programme leader and in serious cases you may be asked to leave the course.

There is an expectation that you attend all your classes. You will be studying on a skills-based course and you need to be able to learn and practise all of the required skills. This provides important reassurance to your future clients. After all, you would not like to visit a hairdresser who had not attended the training sessions for cutting or colouring; you certainly would not like to be operated on by a surgeon who had only completed half of their training. The timetable may leave you with gaps during the day of two or three hours. While this might be a little inconvenient, it also organises space in your day to meet with other students in a study group, arrange appointments with tutors or just give you time to go to the library and read quietly. It should not be seen as time wasted, but as an opportunity.

> 'I'd never really used a library before for formal study. I made time to meet the subject librarian and went to some sessions to find out all of the different services the library could provide. Popping in between lectures helped me to structure any free time and the librarians were so helpful when I needed special books and papers for my dissertation.'

Timetabled sessions are arranged for a particular length of time. Your lecturers will prepare material to best use that time. It will be in your interest to attend the sessions from the beginning in order that you get the most out of them. Arriving late disturbs the class, affects the flow of the session and gives others a wrong impression about you. If you know you are going to be late, do what you can to let the lecturer know. This might mean texting a friend to pass on the message or phoning the lecturer. Some programmes will not allow you into a session once it has started. This may be due to the nature of the session or just out of courtesy to the rest of the group. This may have a longer-term impact on your attendance. Always do your best to get some notes of the sessions you miss.

Books and equipment

On arrival, or perhaps before, you will be inundated with lists of things you will need. This will include a book list. These are provided to give you some indication of the range of books which should be read for your particular course of study. There are books which you have to buy, books which you have to read and books which are recommended for reading. Unfortunately, books are also very expensive and you would expect to pay between £25 and £75 for each text book on the list.

However, it is not essential that you buy every book on the list and the book buying process should be as economical and relevant as possible.

When a friend recommends you read a book it is rare that you do so without considering the advertising, the reviews or the blurb. Often you will pick up the book, flick through its pages and perhaps read some of its content. This should be the same with a text book. Rarely will a text provide you with the only source of information on a topic and it may be that while you find one style of writing difficult to follow, another might explain things in a way which you connect with immediately. There are, for example, many anatomy and physiology text books, each presenting the human body in a slightly different way. The material being considered (the human body) does not change.

Top tips

- Look through several text books on the same subject before selecting any to buy.
- Up to date texts are in the library so you need only buy specialist books about the areas of practice you are interested in.
- Follow the guidance of lecturers when buying text books.

It may also be true that an earlier edition of a text book will have much the same material as the newest edition. The new version may present the material in a different way, have new illustrations and use colour rather than black and white images but the material may be fundamentally the same. In these cases older editions might be bought at a reduced price or easily obtained secondhand. There is often a secondhand book market within the student body of the university. At this point it should also be made clear that as the theory and practice of physiotherapy constantly changes there is a need to update text books. These theoretical developments and adaptations to practice will greatly alter the content of the text book and render previous editions educationally irrelevant except as historical documents. For this reason it is recommended that you discuss the purchase of older books with your tutor who may be familiar with the texts and will be able to offer advice.

Your programme may also require you to have certain pieces of equipment to support your studies. This may be something basic like a set of colouring pencils but you may also be expected to purchase something more expensive such as personal assessment equipment or perhaps clothing. Where these can be bought secondhand, this option might be considered and students further through the programme may be able to assist with this. Some items may be relevant throughout your career and this should also be taken into account.

Induction week

In many ways induction week is the most influential week of your university career. This may be called fresher's week in some institutions or by some programmes. It is usually the first week of the first university term or semester. This is a great opportunity to get to know the university, the staff and the other students with whom you will be spending the next few years of your life. It is often difficult starting out in a new environment but, remember, you will be surrounded by many others who are also making that new start. You are all experiencing this new event together. By making lots of different friends you are more likely to find the people with whom you can work effectively. Try not to become too attached to only one person during this period. While they may be great fun to have around during this introductory week, they may not be the best support when things become more focused and serious later in the year.

There will be some timetabled events during this period when you will complete registrations, sign forms and receive lots of information about the programme. It is likely that you will receive your timetable and direction on the expectations and rules for the programme. The programme team will have spent many hours planning what should be included in this period so it is important that you attend all sessions. This period is also the time when there will be lots of additional activities happening across the university. Local businesses will be trying to attract your custom and may be tempting you with great offers, including free pizza, discounted driving lessons or half price entry. It is sometimes easy to get carried away with all the hustle and bustle of these events. Think carefully before committing yourself to any of these offers. You can always collect the information and go back to them in two weeks when you have had time to think about it.

> 'Even though I was living at home while I was at university, I still felt it was important to go to the events at fresher's week. I joined the physiotherapy society and the Gaelic football team. At the end of my programme I was able to add membership of these groups to my curriculum vitae too.'

The other aspect of fresher's week to consider is the parties. They are on all night, every night, if you read all the flyers you will be given. This is only one week and your finances need to last the year so be wary of spending the next month's rent on one great night. Enjoy yourself but remain in control.

Library facilities

Using the library is one of the most essential skills you need to learn during your studies. When you watch the television quiz *University Challenge* the contestants introduce themselves by indicating they are 'reading' their subject area. This is not said by accident. There is awareness that in order to learn about your subject you need to read about it. The best place for this to happen is in your library. What is great about modern libraries is that they do not consist only of dusty books filling hundreds of shelves; they also have access to millions of electronically published articles. They will also let you access these articles from your own home (although you will need the internet and you do need to follow some rules). Just imagine, you can read almost every article written on physiotherapy without leaving your desk (or even your bed, but that might give the wrong message!). These articles are usually published in professional magazines called journals, which are also made accessible over the internet. Journals provide you with the most up to date information within your academic discipline or profession. Libraries have traditionally held stocks of these journals going back many years and bound together in volumes. Each volume usually contains a year of journals.

In relation to your studies the journals are supported by text books. You will probably be familiar with these. Text books provide an alternative source of information. Unlike journals, a text book can be borrowed from the library. You may be able to borrow ten or more books at a time depending on the policy of the library. The library will never have enough books for every student to have their own copy of every text book so you should seriously consider buying the key text books for yourself or, even better, ask someone else to buy one for you. In order to increase access to text books, libraries are increasingly subscribing to e-books. This gives students electronic access to the content of text books without having to physically hold it. It also means that students can access these books more readily.

The library may also have stocks of video clips, television programmes and music. They will certainly receive the major daily newspapers which give you alternative learning resources. The only way you can get the most out of this is to familiarise yourself with the library as soon as you can. The library will probably run sessions on how to make use of its resources. Get signed up for these early in your programme and find out what to do before you have to prepare your first assignment.

University support

All universities invest in a lot of resources to ensure that students have the most enjoyable and successful experience possible. There is a range of student support services available to try to ensure that students maximise their potential. As students come from a wide variety of backgrounds with a range of life experiences, each brings their own perspective. Your experiences will be very different to those around you and therefore your needs will differ. A university needs to have these services in place to support all their students. It is good to make yourself aware of the potential support on offer in order that you know where to seek help when it is needed. This section will consider a range of services but these will vary from institution to institution.

Academic support

Writing for university can be quite daunting. You may not have experience of working at this level and the university will often have a department which will help you as you try to write your assignments. This may be about constructing your essays, writing in the third person (this is usual practice for most assignments) or perhaps interpreting the questions effectively. They may offer direction to you or perhaps help by proofreading some of your work. While this service does play a key role, remember that your personal tutor or the module team are the best people to discuss your assignments with.

Financial support

While this will be considered in more detail in Chapter 6, remember that the university can only offer support in very limited ways. The university will be able to offer lots of advice to students having financial difficulty. Finance advisers will be available throughout the year to give you advice and information on money matters. This may be about tuition fees, grants, student loans or welfare benefits. The student support team will be able to offer guidance and help with any difficulties which arise.

Student services can also help you to apply to the funding schemes they administer, such as the Access to Learning Fund. The Access to Learning Fund can provide extra help if you're in hardship and need extra financial support. Your university or college will look at your individual circumstances and may be able to help with course or living costs that are not already covered by other forms of financial help –

these could be everyday living costs, childcare costs or support over the summer period, for emergency payments to cover unexpected financial crises or if you are thinking of giving up your course because of financial problems and need extra support to help you keep studying.

Counselling services

Sometimes being away from home, working in a new environment and being put under pressure can be very difficult to cope with. Without the local support of a family and perhaps not having formed strong friendships, this can become more challenging. There is sometimes a concern that expressing doubts and reflecting on personal problems might influence others' attitudes, making some issues too difficult to discuss with a personal tutor. Student support services will provide the opportunity to speak privately with a trained counsellor. This might be used for any aspect of your life and not just the academic demands. As these services are private, the course team will generally have no knowledge of this support unless you wish to disclose it. As with any aspects of your personal life which might impact on your studies, it is advisable that this be mentioned, if not discussed with your personal tutor. This will ensure that you receive the best possible support throughout your studies.

Personal tutors

A personal tutor is the university's attempt to provide you with a best friend. This may sound a little trite but if we look at what they do, you will see why it is crucial to spend time with them. In ideal circumstances you will be assigned a personal tutor during induction week. They will still be working with you after you leave, as they will also provide you with your references when you finally start being interviewed for jobs.

Many students will be leaving home for the first time, and you will be trying to manage yourself for the first time. It is not always convenient or appropriate to speak to someone at home, and they would not necessarily appreciate what university means. This is where your tutor fits in. Whether you are 18 or 58, your tutor will take an interest in your academic development. This might be informally with some occasional discussions about your progress when you or they feel it appropriate. They may wish to formalise this process. This might include a range of meetings throughout the period of your training either as individual one to one sessions or as part of a group of tutees. These meetings will be used to support your academic and personal development while at university. Sometimes these sessions will be used to feed into your personal development portfolio. You may discuss your achievements and the opportunities available to you. You can work together on strategies to make the most of these resources, developing targets and the action plans necessary to achieve them.

Case study: The benefits of a personal tutorial – Laura Hunt

Throughout my degree I have kept a small notebook for each module. This has been very useful to avoid being overwhelmed with new ideas or concerns. I write down new words, areas to further research, assessment questions, incorrect answers on tests and recommended books, journals or websites. I devote time each week to going through my notebooks and research. If after researching I am still unsure of something, I book a tutorial to discuss the subject with a lecturer. This has allowed me to stay organised and in control of my workload. I feel calm that I have made a note about the area and will make time to research or seek further support. Coming prepared to a tutorial with a list of questions saves you time and lets you get the most out of tutorials. Independent learning is the biggest change from sixth form or college to university. Take control of your learning and stay organised with your workload. Do not ignore things you are unsure of as they will continue to pop up and cause undue stress.

Where things are not working well your tutor will also help you to reflect on the experience and consider ways to improve your situation. Remember that your tutor knows about university and its organisation and routines. They understand the student support services and how to read a timetable.

You also need to be aware that your tutor will have other roles. It is not sufficient to turn up at their door and expect half an hour of their time. It may be that you have to email them first or set up a tutorial appointment in order that you can have their full attention. It may be necessary to give them some indication of the nature of your appointment. This will allow your tutor to prepare for the meeting and perhaps book an alternative room to ensure you have privacy. You may also be expected to prepare material for your meeting. You will only get the best out of your tutor if you invest the effort. Having your tutor on your side will certainly make the university experience easier.

Extra-curricular activities

Academic work will take up a large part of your time at university and you should recognise this. This does not, however, prevent you from being involved in other activities or taking on new responsibilities. For some students there will be ongoing family responsibilities which will take precedence over anything else. For many students this will be a time of many new starts. As you make decisions about what you want to do with your time outside of your studies bear in mind that the academic year will have periods when your workload will greatly increase. Part-time work is often a consideration for students. While this is not the ideal situation when studying, it is realistic to acknowledge the necessity of additional income. Bearing this in mind, any potential employer may need to be very flexible. While the timetable may be relatively fixed from week to week, the introduction of your practice placements will commit you to full-time work for a fixed term with the potential for increased travel time. You will also be expected to carry out additional reading or complete projects or presentations which may consume much of your evenings or weekends. This may have an impact on your employment and may need early discussion to avoid longer-term problems.

The students' union and the Chartered Society of Physiotherapy

There are hundreds of students' unions across the country. They are all members of the National Union of Students (NUS). The students' union at your university is there to represent you. It looks after the needs of students in many different ways. In order to get the most out of the union you need to learn more about it, how it can help you and how you can get more involved in running the union yourself. The union exists to improve your experience of university life. It provides welfare services and entertainment such as clubs and bars. Many will also have shops or catering outlets where snacks can be purchased.

Many groups need to have a national voice to ensure there is full representation. The NUS exists to promote, defend and extend the rights of students (NUS, 2012). It fights and campaigns for change with student interests at heart. The union also works on a local level to provide representation for students. This might be through course and faculty representatives; students trained to represent their cohort who meet formally with senior staff from the university to review the programmes and the student experience. They may also flag up unresolved or ongoing issues to university representatives. The union may also offer advisers who can provide independent, professional advice to students when they are having academic problems and where necessary support them in disciplinary hearings held by the university.

The NUS also offers you the NUS extra discount card. For a low annual fee this offers a range of discounts, deals and competitions designed to make student life a little more rewarding. You can use it to make your money go further on books, clothes, sports stuff, CDs, travel, computer gear, gigs, eating out etc. This can also be converted to a PASS card for an additional fee. PASS is the government-accredited scheme for proof of age which works alongside passports and driving licences. Any money spent in the students' union will be put back into student services and helps make the place better for you.

The union also oversees the organisation and management of a number of student societies. These exist to provide opportunities for students to develop new or maintain current hobbies and skills. This might include anything from religious groups to role playing games, from sports to study. You may find your university also includes a physiotherapy society. This will be open to any student in the university and will exist to provide additional learning or social opportunities specifically for the physiotherapist members of the society. This society may also be affiliated to the Chartered Society of Physiotherapy (CSP).

You will need to become a member of the CSP to take full advantage of the support, services and resources. Setting up your CSP student membership is quick and simple. It will take you around ten minutes to complete the documentation. You need to activate your membership on the CSP website to access the resources. Student membership will give you access to a wide range of resources which will help you in your assignments and preparing for practice placements. Being a student member will keep you updated on professional issues. You can also get involved in professional development opportunities that enhance your CV, such as attending events or writing an article for publication. The student membership fee can be paid upfront for the whole of your programme or paid in instalments. Current details can be found on the CSP website.

Chapter summary

Whether this is your first time at university or whether you are returning to complete another degree, it is always important to be prepared as this should help to give you confidence and reduce stress. There are so many different ways to get support while you study and you will find that, rather than being aloof and unapproachable, your lecturers are eager to help you to learn and understand. You just need to let them know that you require some help. Joining your professional body, getting involved in local and national professional events and pacing yourself with your extra-curricular activities will all help make your university years a success.

Key points

- Plan a personal study timetable – if you stick to it this should reduce your stress levels later.

- Don't rush out and buy all the books on the reading list – check first with your personal tutor or the students who are already on the programme.

- Join the Chartered Society of Physiotherapy (CSP) as a student member.

- Go steady in induction week – there is a lot of time left to pay for!

- Make time to learn how the library works and how to get the most from it.

- If you must take on a part-time job ensure your employer understands that you will need time to undertake your practice placements.

Useful resources

Joining CSP as a student member:
http://www.csp.org.uk/membership/join-csp/students/apply-students

National Union of Students: www.nus.org.uk

Student finance and the Access to Learning Fund: www.direct.gov.uk/en/EducationAndLearning/UniversityAndHigherEducation/StudentFinance/index.htm

Reference

National Union of Students (2012) *Who we are*. [Online]. Available from: www.nus.org.uk/en/about-nus/ [Accessed 18 January 2017].

Chapter 6

How do I manage my finances as a student?

A significant issue for individuals considering higher education study is the cost of a chosen programme of study education. The decision to begin a university programme will likely create a situation of debt which you may never have experienced and which you may not be comfortable with. The questions that many potential physiotherapists ask are, 'How will I afford my training?', 'What will I do if I can't pay for the basics like food and rent?' and 'How can I afford a social life?'. Managing your money is an essential part of university life. By making sure your costs are covered you will reduce the risk of getting into financial difficulties later on. Whether you have supported yourself financially for many years, or you're moving out of home for the first time, there are a number of things you might be able to take into account to ensure a degree of financial stability. Most financial advisers will encourage you to use a budget planner to help you budget – good money management will make your student finances last longer and university life less stressful. By considering the ideas presented in this chapter, you may find it easier to support yourself during the course without leaving university with a large burden of debt.

Managing your money during your training is essential. Although there are obvious costs such as accommodation and food, there are many others such as travel, insurance, text books or equipment, bills and leisure activities. You should take time to consider what it is you need, how much it will be, and how you will pay for it. Any budget will consider a number of elements:

- The total income you can expect to receive or savings you can use during the academic year, including:
  - Savings
  - Student loan
  - Grants or bursaries
  - Income from a job

- The details of the essential items you might expect to spend your money on, including:
  - Rent
  - Travel
  - Insurance
  - Car bills
  - Credit card payments
  - Utility bills, for example, water, gas, electricity, if applicable
  - Phone bills and internet
  - TV licence and TV packages
  - Food and drink
  - Laundry costs
  - Council Tax

Once the essential outgoings have been subtracted from the income you can more easily see what money you have left for the extras such as:

- Course books and equipment
- Household goods
- Clothes/shoes
- Toiletries
- Music/films
- Social activities

There will be additional costs subject to your own personal circumstances.

> 'I wasn't so careful with my money in the first term and this caused me problems throughout the rest of that year. My personal tutor pointed me in the direction of student services, where there was a financial adviser who helped me to sort out my money, which helped reduce my stress. I didn't realise how much money I spent on things I didn't need.'

Top tip

The UCAS budget calculator is one of a number of budget calculators available to use in planning your finances. The link can be found at the end of the chapter.

This chapter will now look in detail at some of the key aspects of finance while studying.

Accommodation costs

University accommodation costs vary greatly across the country and are dependent on factors such as geography and the level of facilities provided. Private accommodation is usually the cheapest form of accommodation but is also often of the lowest standard. Universities tend to offer self-catered and catered accommodation which can be more expensive but provide greater quality. Gas and electricity costs and Council Tax are all included in the overall charge for university accommodation whereas these may have to be paid for separately if you rent privately. Once you leave home you will also have to consider protecting your possessions, so it is important that you insure your personal belongings. As you do not own the property you rent it is unnecessary to obtain buildings insurance. You can choose what to cover, such as clothes, TV and phone, and the cost depends on where you are living and what you insure. You can also ask for cover for when you are away from your accommodation, for example if you take your laptop out with you. If you will be living in halls of residence, speak to your accommodation office about their insurance policy.

As a student living in university accommodation you will be exempt from Council Tax. This is also true if you are living in a property which is occupied solely by students. If you are a full-time student and you live with others who are not students then the house will be liable for Council Tax. Your student status may allow the household to get a discount (or an exemption) depending on individual circumstances. Additional information can be found on the Directgov website or from your local council. You will need evidence from your university in order to confirm your student status.

Are there professional costs related to my course?

There are likely to be some additional costs related to your programme of study. How much you pay will depend on you and the programme selected. Membership of the Chartered Society of Physiotherapy (CSP) is one of the costs that you will need to meet. Due to the way some programmes are funded they may pay for this on your behalf. Where this is not the case you will need to meet this cost yourself. The cost of membership is dependent on the total length of your programme and you should visit the CSP website for the current membership fees. It is not essential that you take on this membership but it is a recommendation of your university that you do so and there are many benefits of being a member. Aside from this, there are no other professional costs which all students would be expected to pay.

Individual programmes may introduce additional costs related to the actual programme delivered. This might be to cover materials used in teaching sessions or for extra-curricular learning opportunities. These costs are kept to a minimum and will not have been applied without careful consideration.

Although not technically a professional cost, another cost related to your studies will be in relation to the library. When books are not returned on time there will be fines to pay. These can quickly mount up, so it is worthwhile making sure you only take out the books you need and are likely to use within the period of the loan. Another cost relating to the library is the cost of photocopying, whether this is copying journal articles or pages from books. Although a copy might only be a few pence, this will soon mount up; ten articles of six to seven pages in length will be a few pounds. It is more economical for you to scan the articles and email the scanned document to yourself. This can then be stored on your own computer for access whenever you need it, rather than having to search for a hard copy that you might have mislaid, or perhaps more frustratingly for a single page which has been lost. Depending on the university you attend, you may also have to print out each assignment to submit a paper copy. In addition, you may need to print and bind two copies of the final project or dissertation. You will need to factor in the cost of paper and printer cartridges if you are using your own printer. It is worth remembering that most universities will not allow you to graduate until all of your university accounts (such as course fees, library fines and photocopying bills) have been paid.

Where you can, try to keep costs low, but do not mistake saving money for efficiency as the benefits may be essential to your professional development.

Will I have to pay fees?

From August 2017 new undergraduate physiotherapy students in England will be required to pay for their own training and university fees. This will be funded through tuition and maintenance loans. This funding strategy will apply to postgraduate students from August 2018. This decision will have an impact on training in other areas of the UK. The UK Government continues to consult on funding arrangements for health programmes and these may be subject to change.

Can I obtain a student loan?

This section is not intended to encourage you to take on a loan nor to indicate any preference for a loan or its provider. There are a variety of different loans which a student might be able to access and some of these may be accessible to only some students depending on circumstances. You will be able to apply for the standard student support system provided by the Student Loans Company to cover the cost of your tuition fees and means tested support for living costs. Loan repayments will be the same as those on other non-NHS degree programmes. This means that repayment will start once a graduate is earning £21,000 and repayments are 9% of income over that threshold. This means that a newly qualified band 5 physiotherapist earning £22,000 will pay back approximately £7.50 per month. If the loan has not been paid back after 30 years then the remainder of the loan is written off.

There are two types of loan offered. Tuition fee loans lend up to £9,000 paid directly to the course provider on your behalf. These payments are staged over the year based upon your continuation with the programme. This loan need not be paid until after you have completed the course and in work.

Maintenance loans are also available and these are applied for in the same way. Funds are loaned at the beginning of the term and are means tested subject to your own particular circumstances. This will differ according to whether you are at home or away from home and whether you are living in London or not.

From August 2018 students on the pre-registration Master's courses will also be able to apply for a postgraduate Master's loan. Students can borrow up to £10,000 over the duration of the course to use towards their fees and living costs. As with the other loans, the repayments commence when the £21,000 earnings threshold has been reached. Repayments will be at 6% of income above the threshold and repayments are made alongside repayments of outstanding undergraduate student loans.

In addition to the loans available, students with adult or child dependants can apply for funding in the form of an allowance awarded according to individual circumstances.

A Professional and Career Development Loan may suit your purposes. This might be used to pay for learning that enhances your job skills or career prospects. It can be used for living expenses or to buy books or equipment. This is still a bank loan but the interest on the loan is suspended until one month after the end of your programme. The details for this can be found on the Directgov website.

Case study: Working whilst studying – David Brown

Working while studying may seem a daunting prospect; you might think there are not enough hours or that there will not be enough time to socialise and enjoy student life. You will come to understand that one of the paramount aspects of being a student is mastering the art of plate spinning. The employment plate, however, will crash to the ground in shards of porcelain unless you can exercise the fundamental skill of 'time management'.

When you apply for a job ensure that you are capable of fulfilling it, ideally at the weekends; try to leave the week open to study. If there is an opportunity to take overtime it can be during the week but do not get tied into shifts that will affect your education.

You have to plan ahead; most businesses will give a rota in excess of a fortnight, which should be sufficient to plan your weeks in advance for revision. Mark out on a calendar when you work, study and socialise. Ensure your employer is aware of your placement schedule; some physiotherapy posts are seven-day working and any shifts during this time will need to be negotiated with your employer.

Special needs funding application

If you have a recognised special learning need, perhaps because you have a diagnosis of dyslexia or other disability, then you should ensure that you apply for the funding and support that you are entitled to. Some students do not realise that they have a special need until they have been studying for a while and had some feedback from their tutors. You can still apply for this funding after you have started your programme of study. The support you get depends on your individual needs and not on income. The allowance can help with things such as the cost of specialist equipment or additional travel costs. This is available through the www.gov.uk website or there may be some funding available through your university.

'Although I had an assessment for my learning needs I did not realise that I could apply for additional funding because of this. With the money I was awarded I bought an iPad so that I could easily make notes during sessions and with permission I was able to record the lectures. I got lots of practical support with a notetaker and someone to review my work with me. Through this funding and additional support there was a real difference to my ability to study successfully.'

This may be something you are aware of and can be declared in your application. You may also discuss it with the student support services at the university when you have a confirmed offer of a place. The earlier this is discussed, the more likely it will be that appropriate support and provision will be in place at the beginning of your training.

Chapter summary

Whatever your situation, you will need to have sufficient funds to see you through your time at university. There are some decisions to make about whether to apply for a student loan or perhaps to get a part-time job to supplement your income. There are positive and negative sides to each and it is recommended that you seek financial advice before making any decisions. As well as the funding opportunities already discussed in this chapter, you may be able to secure sponsorship from charities or even the large supermarkets. Some big organisations have sponsorship schemes so it is always worthwhile researching the possibilities and making an application. Remember that banks will also give you student bank accounts, with a variety of incentives for you to choose from. Other student benefits may include (depending on eligibility) free dental treatment and reduced Council Tax. Finally, joining the National Union of Students will allow you to get discounts for admission to films, theatre, National Trust properties and many more places. You'll also get a discount in many stores – which is a bonus, especially at Christmas!

Key points

- Learn how to budget effectively.
- Plan an annual and full course budget.
- Identify potential sources of support before you have financial difficulties.

Useful resources

CSP student membership:
www.csp.org.uk/membership/join-csp/join-student-member

Student finance: www.gov.uk/browse/education/student-finance

Disabled students' allowances:
www.gov.uk/disabled-students-allowances-dsas/how-to-claim

UCAS budget calculator: www.ucas.com/ucas/undergraduate/finance-and-support/budget-calculator

Chapter 7

What do the early years of studying physiotherapy involve?

7: What do the early years of studying physiotherapy involve?

Whenever you commence new studies there will be some anxiety regarding what will be involved and what is expected of you. This is natural and any teaching team will be well placed to acknowledge your concerns and support you throughout the experience. All physiotherapy programmes throughout the UK follow the same curriculum guidelines and have been approved and accredited by representatives of both the Health and Care Professions Council and the Chartered Society of Physiotherapy. This ensures all programmes deliver material of the highest standards, but which is ultimately similar. The difference between programmes is the manner in which that material is organised and delivered. This will be adapted to the interests and the expertise of the teaching team or the facilities available at the university. The course will also be tailored to fully exploit the social and regional context of the programme and the university.

Your programme of studies will have been specifically designed so that you gain the most from the experience. It will be organised to ensure that the things you learn early in the programme will be used as a basis for future learning. This is an essential aspect of higher education and has been developed through many years of teaching and educational research. Your first year will provide you with opportunities to learn more about yourself as well as the profession. You will have opportunities to reflect on your own strengths and the areas in which you feel you could improve. You will also learn what you can achieve and how you might do so. The teaching team will provide you with a range of opportunities to develop your understanding of what physiotherapy is and how physiotherapists view the world. Your programme will allow you to develop an understanding of practices before being asked to apply them in more complex situations. The exception to this is problem-based learning which we have already discussed in Chapter 3.

This chapter will explore some key elements that are frequently delivered in the first year of a physiotherapy programme and will explain some key strategies you could employ to make the most of the learning opportunities.

What skills can I transfer to the programme?

Everyone will enter the programme with some type of formal qualification. A levels (or their equivalent), an Access course or a previous degree will have already developed your study skills which will be very important as you progress through your physiotherapy training.

You will also come to your physiotherapy studies with a range of personal attributes and skills which you have developed throughout your life. It may be that you enjoy undertaking physical activity. Perhaps you are patient and a good communicator and you might want to help people optimise their quality of life. These attributes might have been demonstrated when you applied to university through your personal statement or during the interview process. These skills are highly valued alongside your academic skills.

Because physiotherapists work across a wide range of settings there will be opportunities for you to apply some of your personal skills and previous experience within the university-based programme as well as during your practice placements. These personal attributes enrich the learning experiences of others and will be viewed as being important on the course and welcomed by staff.

Communication skills are important, whether the communication is written in essays and reports or verbal in presentations and discussion with peers. Your ability to work as a team is important as you will be working with groups of other students where you will need to negotiate, delegate tasks and adapt according to the outcome of discussions. This will also include the non-verbal communication we use to support our verbal communication. Typically you will bring skills such as the ability to gather new information and make sense of it, writing reports, managing time and dealing with pressure. Finally you will bring to your studies some computer literacy. It is impossible to be an effective student if you are unable to word process, use journal databases or complete electronic searches on the internet. The university staff and others will contact you via email so it will be important to not only use these skills but also do so in a professional manner.

Do I need to be practical or academic?

Physiotherapy will make a range of demands on you as a student and training is designed to be both academic and practical. This will be combined within the practice placement elements of the programme as you relate the theory learned at university to the practice setting. All students will be expected to demonstrate academic ability as the award of a final degree (or postgraduate qualification) is ultimately based on your ability to achieve satisfactory academic outcomes across the programme. These academic standards are strictly managed and will be rigorously applied through the assessment process and its related quality structures. You will be accepted on a programme because you have already evidenced the academic capacity to be successful, perhaps through your achievements at A level or their equivalents, an Access course or a previous degree. Academic demands will be high but you will have the potential to succeed and will be supported by the university's academic team.

Physiotherapy programmes are very practically focused and you will learn a variety of different physical interventions to improve the functional abilities of your clients on practice placement. You will develop your handling skills within the subjects studied in the early parts of the programme and in particular during anatomy sessions.

Practice placements are a key focus for a student's practical skills. Here you will be given the opportunity to engage in a range of practical activities which will effect change in the clients you work with. The practical skills demanded of you will not require you to have prior expertise in this area but you may need to be able to replicate the skills of your educator. It is more important that you are observant and willing to take part. Further discussion of placements follows in Chapter 8.

Topics covered

Anatomy and physiology

Anatomy and physiology are the underpinning biological sciences within physiotherapy and are studied in depth in the early years of physiotherapy programmes. Human anatomy is the study of the structure of the human body, whereas human physiology is the branch of science that involves the study of the function of the human body. Within physiotherapy the study of anatomy and physiology would concentrate on the musculoskeletal, neurological and cardiorespiratory systems. The anatomy and physiology of the musculoskeletal system would involve bones, joints, muscles and also connecting tissues such as ligaments. Study of the nervous system would focus on the structure and function of the brain, spinal cord and also the nerves of the peripheral nervous system which supply your muscles and other organs. The anatomy and physiology of the cardiorespiratory systems involves the heart, lungs and blood vessels which would supply your organs and body structures with blood.

Academic staff will use a variety of learning strategies to develop your knowledge of anatomy and physiology. These could include lectures, seminars, laboratory/practical classes and also the use of digital and multimedia resources. The best way to learn anatomy and physiology is practically and it would be expected that there would be a significant number of practical and laboratory classes within the early years of a physiotherapy programme.

Physiotherapy assessment, intervention and evaluation

In order to be an effective physiotherapist and physiotherapy student you will need to be able to identify clients' problems, select the appropriate treatments or interventions and evaluate how successful they have been. In the early stages of the programme you will develop an understanding of the principles of a physiotherapy assessment for clients with problems of the musculoskeletal, cardiovascular and respiratory and neurological systems. You will also learn about a range of conditions which you may see on practice placement. These conditions will be across the lifespan, enabling you to gain insight into commonly experienced problems by children and adults. You will also learn physiotherapy treatment interventions which would include movement and exercise, manual therapy and education and advice. Learning how your interventions have been successful are an important part of evidence-based practice and you will have an opportunity to learn how to evaluate yourself and your interventions.

Research

Throughout your life you have been exposed to research. If you have read the ingredients on a breakfast cereal box or looked at a bus timetable you have undertaken research and in your previous studies this will have been formalised in some way. Your training as a physiotherapist will advance your understanding of research. In the early part of your programme you will be exposed to research in a range of situations and you will learn about certain methodologies, how they work and where they will be most effectively used. Qualitative and quantitative methods will be explored and strategies for their application will be discussed. It is also likely that you will discuss the limitations of these research methods to avoid their use in inappropriate situations.

Research will be found in all your text books and make up the majority of articles in the journals which will underpin your assignments and learning. You will be directed to this research and expected to read it and understand it. This is an essential part of developing the skills for locating data and a practical teaching method to equip you with skills for study and for functioning as a physiotherapist. To exploit this it is advisable that you spend time talking with the staff in the library who are the real experts in finding this material and who will be happy to teach you. In the early stages of your training you will learn how to use evidence to substantiate your arguments and to introduce debate and critique to your work. In later years you will analyse and synthesise this material into your academic work and use this to validate your placement endeavours.

We all expect to have the very best care that is available and this can only be achieved when research is undertaken. Within healthcare this is presented through the notion of evidence-based and evidence-informed practice. In other words, we identify through research the very best strategies for intervention and then use this evidence to direct our practice as physiotherapists. These are important concepts in healthcare and will influence your studies and subsequent practice.

Practice placement

Early in your training as a physiotherapist you will have the opportunity to experience a practice placement. This will be discussed in detail in Chapter 8 but it is useful to realise that this experience will only be a snapshot of what physiotherapy is. While many students find placements stimulating and enjoyable, occasionally students embarking on their studies become disillusioned in their first practice experience because they gain an alternative understanding of physiotherapy and this does not equate with their previous expectations. It is advisable to consider the role of the physiotherapist in a variety of situations before you commence training in order that you avoid this potential difficulty while also preparing you more effectively for application forms and interviews.

If this does happen to you, do not make snap decisions and withdraw from the programme. It is unlikely that you will have the same placement experience again and if this is an area you find particularly difficult then it is unlikely that you will take up future employment in this field. It is not necessary to enjoy all aspects of physiotherapy practice to be a physiotherapist – but you must be able to understand a wide range of therapeutic contexts and interventions. Your placement educators or university tutors will be happy to listen to your concerns and discuss them with you.

Your programme will offer a range of learning opportunities for you to prepare fully for placement. This will review elements such as placement documentation, teach you negotiation skills and train you in the practical skills of moving and handling. Learning these skills will allow you to maximise the learning potential of your practice placements.

Getting the most out of lectures

Lectures are the educator's way of getting the most information to the greatest number of people. They are used to introduce a topic to a group of students but will not provide all the answers. A lecture can be seen as a way of transferring the ideas in a text book into something which is meaningful and relevant to the student. It will usually identify and bring to your attention the key ideas or debate relating to the subject matter, applying examples and explanations to the theoretical ideas of the topic. You will be signposted to influential thinkers in a topic and relevant texts and source material will be indicated. As a student you should be thinking about how this information might be relevant to your previous study and the implications for practice.

In order to make the most of this you should be preparing for every lecture. Where possible, many programmes will place copies of lecture materials on the university intranet pages, where they can be read beforehand or even downloaded and taken along to the session to support the presentation. This will help you to become familiar with the topic so that you can then focus on what is being said rather than copying the presentation. The notes you make are very important. Try to develop a note keeping system that will provide you with the best material. This is not about copying every word; rather, it is about being selective in what you write. It may be necessary for you to develop your own abbreviations which would allow you to make notes more effectively, or perhaps you could use spider diagrams or mind maps to organise the material in a way which differs from just writing down every word. Some students try to avoid taking notes by recording the lecture. While this frees you up to listen more carefully, due to time constraints students often do not listen to this material again. It is useful to view the recording as a backup only.

When you have obtained your material from the lecture go back through it and try to organise your thoughts. You are likely to have forgotten most of the material discussed within a week so it is important that you make your material accessible. Highlight areas for additional consideration and use your study time to review this material and consolidate your knowledge.

Top tips

- Prepare for lectures by reading around the subject before going into the lecture.
- If there are lecture slides available, review them before the lecture in order that you can make notes on the additional material being shared, rather than copying the projected slides.

Getting the most out of seminars

Seminars give students the opportunity to work on the practical aspects of the theory they have learnt. They are also a forum in which to develop discussion and presentation skills. Seminars usually involve the discussion of material presented in a lecture or in directed reading, exploring it in more detail than the lecture allows. You will be working in groups and often this will allow you to listen to and question the ideas shared by group members, giving you additional perspectives and insights into the subject material. It will also give you the opportunity to receive criticism and defend your own ideas. This may cause some anxiety and this is not uncommon. Many students do not like sharing their views openly or challenging other people's ideas. This can be embarrassing but can be managed. With thorough preparation you are more likely to be confident with the material you present.

You will get the most out of seminars if you prepare for them. Review the material you need for the seminar – you may have some directed reading or perhaps only the seminar title but you can use this to read around the subject. It will be useful if you have some ideas which you can introduce, or perhaps there are questions you need to have answered.

> 'I really enjoyed the seminars because it gave me the chance to ask questions and to learn in a practical way. We were in different groups each year, so I got to study with lots of different people.'

As you participate in the session remember that you are there to learn as well as putting your ideas forward. Listening is an important skill and is very useful as you consider new subjects. Other people will offer alternative perspectives or will have read useful material that will increase your understanding of the subject so take notes on things being said. It is not just the tutor that will have something valuable to say; other students might also have some relevant comments and it is useful to write things down that are of interest. If there is something you do not understand ask about it and talk it through with the rest of the group. As others become involved in the discussions you have during these sessions you will develop your skills in group work and in presenting your material to others.

Sometimes the idea of speaking out in a group of people that you do not know well may cause anxiety but there are some strategies you can employ beforehand which will help you to deal with these feelings. Get to know the other group members, so that you feel more at ease. This will help the seminar feel like a discussion among friends. It may also be appropriate to challenge yourself to ask a question or make a contribution in each session to build your confidence. Participation does not require you to take over the session but to make a brief and relevant point or to respond to someone else's questions. Remember that seminars are there to help you learn, not for you to show how much you know.

Case study: Getting the most out of taught sessions – Sara Edwards

Teaching sessions, whether they are practical sessions or seminars, are designed to make you think on your feet by giving you scenarios you have never seen, usually simulating something you may see on placement. The lectures also allow you to develop transferable skills or your own clinical reasoning, or to practise hands-on skills. Before lectures there is often guided reading to do to get background on what you will be covering in the lectures. The benefit of this is to allow you to read around and create your own notes as not everything can be covered during lectures. During sessions, theory and practical are mixed to allow you to understand how the theory relates to the practical. Practical sessions help the development of skills (such as handling and communication) and allow you to receive feedback on your approach to a model from the lecturer.

From my own learning, taught sessions have helped me develop a baseline for placement preparation. This gives a chance to establish a strong background before commencing placements and also allows for any questions to become more focused whilst on the placement, rather than being general.

Tutorials move the focus for learning from the educator to the student. This can be quite intimidating for a student, at least in the beginning. Tutorials usually take place in small groups or perhaps as one to one sessions. They give students access to academic staff for focused teaching in particular subjects or support in managing their learning. In terms of learning the tutorial system can be very rewarding but it does make great demands on the student.

In traditional teaching the teacher is seen as the person who teaches and this is the role of lectures and seminars. The tutorial should allow you to use your tutor as a mentor who assists you in your development as a student and will aid you in more autonomous learning. Although you will have support from your tutor you need to recognise that you should be completing work independently outside of the timetabled sessions. The tutorial should give you the opportunity to review and critically discuss the material you have been considering both in the taught sessions and in your self-directed reading.

Getting the most out of practical/laboratory classes

Practical classes are an integral part of your learning experience as you will need to be able to apply your theoretical knowledge of anatomy and treatment interventions. You will be able to do this in a safe environment to try out your skills before undertaking these on practice placement. Hopefully your confidence will increase through your own active participation and the opportunity to work closely with your peers. Another benefit is the opportunity to experience how closely physiotherapists work with their clients, which involves a hands-on approach. For these sessions male students may be required to wear shorts and female students are usually expected to wear shorts and a sports bra. Your lecturers will be sensitive to any cultural requirements. While this may be embarrassing at first you will soon get used to this way of learning and students value the different opportunities that these classes bring.

Other learning opportunities

University will offer other learning opportunities. This might include workshops or other practical sessions. These sessions will offer you the opportunity to try things out for yourself. Whether these are compulsory sessions in moving and handling, the control of infection, or perhaps the use of treatment media, you will be learning how to actually complete the practical task. You will generally be facilitated through this process by a member of academic staff who will guide you through the procedure and offer suggestions on how to remember important details or techniques. You may have the opportunity to act as the client or the therapist in order that your colleagues can develop their skills. This will help you to begin to appreciate what a client may be experiencing if they were to participate in this task. It is often worth reflecting on these workshop experiences and using the opportunity as a springboard for additional learning.

Chapter summary

The first year of your programme will be exciting, tiring and fulfilling. As each week passes by you will learn more and feel increasingly able to piece information together to improve your understanding. There will be emotional highs and lows. Remember that all students experience this and that you are not alone. Take time at the end of the year to look back and reflect on everything you have learned. As well as refreshing your memory it will help you to celebrate how far you have progressed.

Key points

- At the beginning everyone will be new to the course – so you are all facing similar challenges.
- Plan for lectures, seminars and tutorials to ensure you are prepared.
- Read around the subjects to widen your knowledge and understanding.
- Be an active participant in your learning – don't just sit back and let others do the work.

Useful resources

An interesting article and links relating to Kolb's experiential learning: Smith, M. K. (2001, 2010) David A. Kolb on experiential learning. *The Encyclopedia of Informal Education.* [Online]. Available from: http://infed.org/mobi/david-a-kolb-on-experiential-learning/ [Accessed 20 December 2016].

Chapter 8

Physiotherapy practice placements

Most students are eager to go out on their first practice placement and positive feedback about practice placements is very common on the end of course evaluations. So, what are placements all about?

What does being on practice placement mean?

A practice placement is the opportunity to try out in practice the theory you will have been learning in university. Each university programme will have different combinations of practice placement, with placements of different lengths, at different stages in the programme and with different marking criteria. When you are looking at which programmes to apply to, you should consider the practice placements as this may have an effect on your choice of programme.

When you start your training you will be told all about the practice placements at your university. All universities endeavour to provide students with a variety of placements in order to ensure every student has a broad range of experiences. The availability of placements depends on whether practice placement educators are available to take students. It is a complex task to allocate the right student to the right placement at the right time, and most universities will have a practice placement tutor who co-ordinates all of this. In order for you to be able to plan properly for your placement, you will be given advance notice of where you will be going and who will be your educator.

It is your responsibility to contact the placement co-ordinator or educator in a timely way, to introduce yourself and to make any plans for your first day. You'll need to remember that, if you don't write until the last minute or if you send only a cursory note, this will be the first impression you give of yourself to the person who will be supervising and assessing your performance. Before going on practice placement you will need to have attended a substantial amount of theory lectures, seminars and practical skill classes at university. All of your module work leading up to your placements is designed to give you the best theoretical knowledge and practical skills in order that you can put these into practice. You will also have had the opportunity to think about practical issues, such as infection control, moving and handling, communication skills, lone working, consent and confidentiality. You should be given information regarding the kind of clothes to wear, whether this is your student uniform or smart casual clothes, and information about jewellery, tattoos and body odour (yes, even that) and you should use this information to plan for your first day.

Case study: Student experience of practice placement – Emma Wortley

Year 1 practice placement is daunting. Well, for someone like me anyway. I'm that student that doesn't have any confidence in her own ability and is convinced that she never does anything right. Rocking up to my first day of three weeks in musculoskeletal outpatients, my stomach was churning, palms sweating, I was so nervous! Looking back now, I have no idea why I was so stressed, I absolutely loved it. I felt part of the team from day one and was able to observe things I never thought I would get the chance to as a first year student. By the time three weeks was up, I had overcome my fear of talking to patients and manual handling, and was conducting subjective assessments unsupervised, directing objective assessments and treating my own patients. Who would have thought? Certainly not me. I was thrown out of my comfort zone and grew not only as a person, but as a clinician, gaining tonnes of confidence and self-belief. My knowledge base expanded, I learnt how to navigate the computer system and write patient notes, I came across pathologies I had never heard of before and I got the chance to work alongside some amazing physiotherapists.

What activities will I undertake?

This will depend on the placement and your level of study and competency. Each placement will have been graded so that you have the opportunity to develop your skills and reach higher goals on each subsequent placement. You will not be expected to know everything on your first placement – but by the end of year three there will be an expectation that you can work independently.

Some universities may have the first placement as an observation placement, where you are given the opportunity to shadow the physiotherapists to see what they do. Even on this placement you will be involved in carrying out some activities, for example writing up what you have seen and heard, attending case conferences and assisting with assessments and treatments.

Other universities may no longer have an observation placement and will expect you to participate in many more activities even on a first placement. Remember that when each programme is planned the academic staff will have thoroughly considered the information that they will need to teach you before going on placement in order for you to do this. This ensures that you are not dropped in from a great height without any sort of safety net!

You will be expected to undertake activities that fit with your level of training, both with and without supervision. Some students are reassured that their educator is with them when they try things for the first time and others feel better having a go before someone observes them – you should communicate with your educator to ensure they are aware of your preferred learning style. In order for your educator to make an informed decision about your competency, however, they will need to observe you undertaking the tasks at some point. This isn't to catch you out; it is to ensure you are safe.

There are lots of activities that you might be involved in, depending on the type of placement you are undertaking. At the very least, you will be assessing people's ability, communicating with many different people, planning physiotherapy interventions, carrying them out and evaluating their outcome. The list is endless, so be open minded and learn from everything that you have the opportunity to do. You will be expected to be enthusiastic, to seek out learning opportunities and to be forthcoming in your discussions about how and what you have been learning. Remember that you will need to demonstrate your learning to your educator, by either showing them or telling them.

What hours will I work?

In total you need to complete 1,000 hours of practice placement, spread over the duration of your training programme. Each placement will be of a particular length and may have a small number of extra hours added to ensure that the placement is still viable if you are unable to go in for whatever reason. You will be expected to work full time during your practice placement, even if your educator is part time. Most universities allow for half a day personal study time in each week of placement and in most cases it will be up to you to negotiate this time with your educator. In the majority of cases, placements happen from Monday to Friday; however, there are many services that are now operating seven days a week and you may be asked to work the same shift pattern as your educator, which may include some weekend work. Additionally, you may need to stay in hospital accommodation for the duration of your placement as the placement site may be some distance from the university.

Do I wear uniform?

You will be informed by the university about the uniform requirements and how to order what you need. Hopefully, as long as you stay the same size for the whole of your programme, you will not need to buy any extra uniform! Many hospitals have a policy of having arms bare below the elbows (for hygiene reasons) and some hospitals are not keen to have staff with visible tattoos – so you may wish to check this out before making your application.

For health and safety reasons you will be asked to refrain from wearing jewellery – watches, badges, rings, piercings – as these can harm patients during moving and handling procedures or could be a danger for you if someone chose to pull on them.

Whether you wear uniform or not, you will need a sensible pair of shoes, as you will be surprised how much you will be on your feet during the working day. Health and safety suggests a proper shoe where your toes are covered.

If you do not need to wear a uniform on placement you will be expected to wear smart, casual, clean clothes. Men are advised not to wear a tie unless it is a clip-on tie, and again, the same points about jewellery and shoes should be noted. You need to remember that you are representing your profession so you need to look professional. Although in the summer you might wish to be wearing a strappy T-shirt or sleeveless vest, the clients you are going out to see may not find it comfortable to see an expanse of cleavage or hot underarms! Likewise with trousers, you are strongly advised not to wear the modern style that sit across the hips. This is because when you bend over (which you undoubtedly will do) you will instantly reveal an expanse of your bottom that no self-respecting professional would want to show to their service user. Commonly referred to as 'builder's bottom', this can be avoided by wearing trousers that sit firmly around your waist.

Although it is unlikely that you will have to regularly wear your uniform at university, the same considerations about dress should be considered, especially if you are doing practical sessions.

Will I get support?

Support is normally offered to you in a number of ways while you are out on practice placement, depending on the university you attend.

You will be allocated a practice placement educator who you will work alongside and who will usually be your first port of call in any given situation. These educators will, in the majority, have completed an accreditation course in order to demonstrate their competence to educate students. They will have attended taught sessions at a university and have had their work assessed – on top of which they will have had experience working in their speciality as well as having educated students. They too have been student physiotherapists and understand the stresses and pressures that some students may feel on placement. They give their time to help students get the valuable experience they need to put theory into practice. You should be offered an opportunity to have some protected time with this person for your supervision each week – but most educators will make it clear that you don't have to wait until that session if you have a concern that you need to discuss.

There may also be a placement co-ordinator in the organisation that you are on placement in, who may be able to offer support. You will also be offered informal support from the other staff you will be working alongside. A member of academic staff from the university may also be allocated to you as the person who will either come out to visit you halfway through your placement or give you a phone call. This is a way to offer you support and ensure that you are meeting the objectives of the placement. They can facilitate discussions between you and your placement educator, listen to your concerns and help you to decide how to move forward with any issues you feel you have. They will listen to the feedback your placement educator gives to you and will offer advice and suggestions where required. Some universities have a dedicated team purely for practice placement supervision, so you may be allocated to the same academic for all of your placements. Whatever the situation, you will have support from the university because your personal tutor is always contactable should you need to speak with them.

Some larger placement providers are able to set up student support groups if they have a group of students at the same time. There may be educational seminars, staff meetings or learning sets available for students to attend too. All placement educators and academics will say that it is so much easier to support a student if the student is open and honest about any difficulties they may be having, whether it is at the placement or something happening outside that may be affecting their work. The sooner you enlighten someone about a problem the sooner it can be resolved, so you should never be worried about speaking to someone.

How will I be assessed?

Some universities base the placement assessment on a pass/fail basis, with the educator making this decision, while other universities ask the educator to give a numerical mark or a grade, linked to the university marking criteria. This information may help you to decide which university you wish to attend, as having a numerical mark or grade may make a difference to your degree classification at the end of your programme.

Whichever method is used, each programme will have an assessment form for the educator to fill in. You may be involved in this too. Some forms are written and some include a visual analogue scale, where progress is indicated on a continuum.

You will need to be able to demonstrate your competency against the criteria on the form. The criteria will link to the Standards of Proficiency of the Health and Care Professions Council and the Chartered Society of Physiotherapy Professional Standards.

There is an expectation that you, along with your educator, will establish weekly objectives for the duration of the placement. Each week the objectives should enable you to demonstrate your learning towards the end goal of achieving the competencies. You will have the opportunity to discuss your progress each week in your supervision sessions. It is very important that you ensure that you have prepared for these sessions and that you take along all the evidence you need to support your claims of competency. If your educator has asked you to undertake a piece of work this should also be available for them to view. Equally important will be a reflection on your learning over the preceding time. This will help to show your educator how you have reviewed your opportunities, what you have learned from them and how you plan to develop.

If you are not achieving your objectives then your educator will point this out to you. They will give you examples of how you could improve and they will expect to see you put this into action. Remember that their feedback is given to you in order to help you to be as good as you can be and so you should try to accept this information with humility and a positive attitude. If you do not demonstrate an improvement or if your educator has a serious concern about your ability to practise, they will contact the university to discuss the options with your practice placement academic or personal tutor. It may be that they are able to agree an action plan over the telephone or the academic may feel it is more appropriate for them to come out to do an on-site visit. This is always meant in a supportive way, with everyone trying to help you to achieve the right level of competency. If you are not able to make the required changes, however, your educator may feel that you have failed to meet the competencies and your report will reflect this. Depending on your past record on practice placement, you may or may not be offered the opportunity to re-sit the placement, usually in a different service. Universities will only allow a student to fail two practice placements over the duration of a programme – if a student were to fail a third placement then this would result in them being asked to leave the programme. You will need to check the university policy on this before you decide which university to attend.

Professional suitability is a responsibility of all physiotherapists and student physiotherapists. Students must be deemed to be professionally suitable to pass their placement.

What about my safety?

Prior to your placement you will undertake any specialist training that your programme deems reasonable for your safety. Although you may have read or heard about incidents involving patients and staff, the number of incidents is extremely low and the majority of staff will have a long career without witnessing any incidents. What is most important is to recognise that if activities are planned using up to date information and with reference to reducing risks then the likelihood of an unsafe situation is minimised.

All placement establishments are required by the universities to be audited to ensure that they have the correct safety procedures in place. Fire, basic life support and first aid, lone working and manual handling procedures are essential. Many universities will provide training in manual handling techniques for students as well as offering the opportunity for students to undertake conflict resolution training.

Where students are placed on placements in a secure setting, training will be provided by the placement to ensure students are aware of their responsibilities as well as the rules and safety precautions already in place. It is important to know that as a student you will be less likely to be left by yourself in any situation until your educator has had an opportunity to make an assessment about how you will cope. Harassment, whether verbal or physical, is not tolerated in any workplace, and there will be policies and support available for students. You should not be asked to undertake any task which is unsafe or beyond your competence.

While on placement you are covered by insurance, the detail of which will be explained by the placement team. You may need to increase your own car insurance if you will be expected to use your own car while on placement; however, a car is not a requirement of all placements and again, this will be something you will want to discuss with the university placement team or tutor.

Case study: Non-traditional placement: Women's Health – Alys Roberts-Garland

I was lucky enough to be given the opportunity to have a placement within Women's Health which is a specialised area of physiotherapy practice with very few expert qualified practitioners. Women's Health covers both inpatient and outpatient care. On the mornings, I had outpatient clinics where women of all ages, especially those who had recently given birth or had gynaecological surgery, would seek advice on how to control or improve their bladder and bowel habits. This included giving exercises, programmes, dietary and lifestyle advice. Pregnant ladies also came into clinic who had back pain or were struggling with their walking as the normal MSK outpatients for the general public do not specialise in pregnancy related conditions. Once assessed there were many treatment options available which were chosen based on the patient's individual problem list which may have included massage, stretches, strengthening exercises, education on gait (walking) technique, issuing walking aids such as crutches, and lifestyle and exercise advice.

In the afternoon, I went onto the gynaecological wards and maternity wards to give patients post-surgery or post-birth advice on activities of daily living and exercises to complete at home before they were discharged home. The ward environment enabled me to develop many skills, including respiratory to check patients' chests were clear post-operations, and gave me the opportunity to work with many other professionals including midwives alongside whom physiotherapists do not always have the chance to work. I really enjoyed this placement; it offered variety and has broadened my knowledge on the role of a physiotherapist outside our traditional role whilst helping to increase my knowledge and confidence on assessment, problems and treatment techniques to a different cliental group.

What is an elective placement?

Some universities may have an elective placement as part of the programme. This is normally a placement that you will arrange yourself and could include the NHS, private practice, social care settings, the voluntary sector and also overseas. Some universities provide this opportunity to enable students to try a particular area of practice that might not normally be available regularly for students. It also gives a student the opportunity to work in an area of practice that they may eventually wish to work in. This will give them the chance to see if it is all they had imagined it to be. There may still need to be some negotiation with the placement team or tutor, to ensure the placement is suitable and that the practicalities such as insurance are covered.

Is there an opportunity to study overseas?

There may be an opportunity for you to undertake a placement overseas; indeed many students take the opportunity to plan an elective placement abroad. Of course, this is likely to take more planning on your part, but the students who the authors have known who undertook an overseas placement had nothing but praise for the experience. If this will be an important feature of the programme that you wish to apply for, then you should make sure you ask the admissions tutor about the possibilities and opportunities.

Chapter summary

Going on practice placement can be exciting and daunting at the same time. It is an opportunity for you to put into practice the theory you have been learning and, for many students who like to learn in a practical way, this is the opportunity to do just that. Getting to know your supervisor before you go on placement is an advantage, as it means you have one less person to introduce yourself to on your first day. Good planning is essential as well as having an open mind. Ask relevant questions at suitable times and make the most of every opportunity. After all, you may decide to apply for a post in the placement area after you graduate and you'll want the staff to remember you from your placement for all the right reasons!

Key points

- Plan for your placement by reading about the conditions you are likely to be treating.
- Contact the relevant practice staff early and in a professional manner.
- Follow the policies and procedures at all times.
- Don't be afraid to ask questions – your placement educator will expect you to do this.

Useful resources

The Chartered Society of Physiotherapy: www.csp.org.uk

The Health and Care Professions Council: www.hcpc.org.uk

HCPC Standards of Proficiency:
www.hpc-uk.org/assets/documents/10000DBCStandards_of_Proficiency_Physiotherapists.pdf

Chapter 9

What do the final years of studying physiotherapy involve?

The final year of the programme will come around all too fast. In this chapter we will discuss how to plan for the final year and consider some of the opportunities and assessments that you might expect to encounter.

It will be tempting over the preceding summer holiday to make the most of the last long summer break you might have for a while; however, it is also a time that could be used to prepare yourself for the final modules. If you plan your time in advance you can have a balanced summer and return to your programme feeling refreshed and prepared. So, what are you preparing for? The final year is the opportunity for you to demonstrate how all of the theory you have so far learned about fits into contemporary practice. There will be a mixture of theory and placements and a final project or dissertation to complete.

As soon as you are notified of the timetable it is wise to plan your self-directed study time around this. Put time aside for each module and remember to check the dates that are published for the submission of assignments. Plan in any essential family or personal activities and time that you will rest. It might feel overorganised; however, planning ahead should reduce some of the stress later. The final year is not the year to attempt without preparation. Your degree classification will depend on the marks you receive in this year.

Is there a dissertation to write?

There will be different requirements regarding the final large assignment for each individual programme. In order to be awarded the 'Honours' element of any BSc programme a final dissertation or project must be undertaken and passed. The Honours element of the programme is essential for any student wishing to register with the Health and Care Professions Council as a physiotherapist – without this it is not possible to register and practise. Within MSc programmes a dissertation or research-based assignment will be required; however, many of these programmes allow students the opportunity to 'step off' at Postgraduate Diploma (PgDip) level, which would still allow them to practise as a physiotherapist.

A dissertation is the opportunity for students to demonstrate in one assignment the culmination of all their learning. There is preparation for the task through various research methods modules and no one is expected to automatically know how to complete the assignment. The dissertation may be primary or secondary research, carried out as individual students or in a small team and then written up as individual projects. Some programmes ask students to undertake a final project rather than a traditional dissertation. The size of the piece of work is similar but may be in the form of an extended research proposal, a business case or perhaps a service improvement plan.

With these large assignments, students are most usually allocated a supervisor from the academic staff team, who will support them throughout the activity. This supervisor will offer guidance, in line with university policies, on the academic element of the assignment as well as from a pastoral point of view. Some students do find this final assignment more of a challenge, mainly as it has been built up to be (through hearsay mainly) a difficult assignment to undertake. Academic staff will reassure students that the work is most certainly achievable if the student starts the work as soon as it is allocated, has a sound work plan and seeks support as soon as any issues arise. Many programmes offer a wide range of other methods of support, from comprehensive work books and module guides to access to research methods staff, e-learning resources and the opportunity to participate in group supervision. Group supervision has been shown to help to motivate students to get on with the work as they are prompted to do so by comparing their progress with that of their peers.

Case study: Writing a dissertation – Kirsty Eason

Having completed two dissertations, one for my BSc (Hons) and one for my MSc, I can safely say the hardest part is picking your topic and phrasing your research question. After that there is a vast range of books and research to help guide you. A dissertation is a brilliant opportunity to look at your area of interest in depth and learn a range of transferable skills that are attractive to employers. I chose to do qualitative research on both occasions and gained valuable interview, writing and critical analysis skills.

There are challenges and stressful moments where you are very aware of the deadline looming or the vast amount of words unwritten. However, the benefits far outweigh the challenges. Actually finishing a substantial piece of work that you have put a lot of effort into gives a great sense of accomplishment. The best advice I can give is to have a plan, attempt to be organised and utilise the valuable experience of your research tutor. There was the option of not completing a dissertation when undertaking my course. I chose to complete the dissertation because I wanted to gain the MSc and because my research topic is important to me. I have seen the remarkable difference it can make to people's lives and so providing an evidence base is vital to ensuring its continued success and funding. One day I hope to see my name published in a journal and I know the skills I learned while completing my dissertation will be what helps to make that possible.

9: What do the final years of studying physiotherapy involve?

These large assignments may have additional elements to them as well as having a large expected word count. Most Master's level dissertations will also involve a *viva voce*, where the work is presented to a small panel who will ask questions about the various elements of the work. Some final projects will involve this too. Often there is a requirement to produce a poster or electronic poster around which the presentation will take place. The panel will usually comprise at least one academic staff member plus one or more of the following people: clinical staff, service users, students or external examiners.

> 'This may sound strange, but I really enjoyed presenting my dissertation. It felt like all of my hard work was being admired and because I knew my topic in so much depth, it was easy to answer any questions!'

This is the student's opportunity to demonstrate their knowledge of the subject they have just spent months studying and should help to give them the confidence to go on to submit their work for peer review to their peers at a conference or other proceedings. Many students do this and it is a joy to listen to the findings of their work.

Will there be option modules?

Some programmes may offer final year students the opportunity to study a particular area of practice in more depth via an optional module. Where this is available students can develop their skills in a particular area of practice or management. Option modules may also be offered at other times in the programme but tend to be scheduled later on as they are usually building on the core material that has been delivered earlier in the programme. It is useful to know that even mandatory modules in a final year are often more flexible in the way work is undertaken. In many cases the assignment brief entails the student choosing an essay title, selecting an area to undertake an elective or role emerging placement and deciding on a topic for their dissertation or final project. In this way, students are given the opportunity to develop areas of interest. It is useful to discuss your ideas with your personal tutor to ensure that you are not choosing topics that are too similar. It would not be sensible to undertake all your third year assignments around one condition or client group, as this may lead you to have too narrow a learning experience.

In addition to this, some programmes offer students the opportunity to participate in an Erasmus+ exchange. This is where students are able to study abroad in a partner university or practice placement. Each programme has different opportunities available to students. If the opportunity to study abroad is one of the key requirements on your list then you should remember to check the up to date details of each available educational programme online and then contact the admissions tutor to confirm that these opportunities are still available.

Finally, some programmes offer students the opportunity to undertake additional training free of charge. It might feel like this could put extra pressure on the final year student; however, it is certainly worth considering all the opportunities available. Some examples of additional training worth consideration are the European Computer Driving Licence or a British Sign Language qualification. Most universities also provide free or low cost summer school places for existing students, so it is worthwhile looking at these opportunities too. Look out for courses that other schools or faculties are running as well as the health and social care opportunities. You may find that the Business School or faculty within the university can offer useful short courses on business planning, accounting and other useful skills for the individual who may be keen to set up in independent practice. Another useful contact will be the Enterprise department, which will be able to advise you on extra support if you have a new business solution or an idea for a new piece of technology or equipment that you would like to develop.

Preparing for practice

The final year of study offers the opportunity to develop the additional skills required for the competent practitioner. Up to this point there will have been a great number of skills to learn that have been directly linked to practice with service users. There is a raft of other professional skills that students will be given the opportunity to develop ready to transition from being a student to being an independent practitioner.

Many final year students contemplate how different it will be to have to take full responsibility for their actions when they qualify. This is because even though there has been a steady progression during practice placements from being a novice to becoming competent in the final placement objectives, there will have always been a practice educator or supervisor around to check each unknown with. Some students express a view that as students they didn't feel it was their place to challenge other staff when something didn't seem quite right because they were 'just a student'. The realisation that this will not be an acceptable reason for non-action looms heavy and some students feel concerned about whether they will be assertive when the situation calls for it. In addition to this, students need to be able to begin to trust in their own intuition and reasoning skills in order to build their self-confidence. This should be facilitated through the practice placement element of the programme as well as through the final year assignments but there will be other opportunities for the proactive student to test themselves out before they complete the programme.

At the beginning of the final year it is essential to reflect upon the skills already learned and those that are yet to be addressed. Carrying out a simple SWOC (strengths, weaknesses, opportunities and challenges) analysis and then linking this to a learning contract should help to add some structure to your self-development. A learning contract is a formal document you might develop with your tutor, which will identify areas for development and learning. It should include areas for development, resources to be used and a timescale for completion. By this time in your training you will have developed the ability to look widely for learning opportunities, so the learning contract will be an in-depth document that guides you towards a variety of ways to validate your learning. It is certainly a document that you can use when meeting with your personal tutor to discuss your progress. Networking opportunities are invaluable and there are often student conferences and study days available at low cost. If your own university has a student group then this is certainly something you should be actively involved in during your final year, as there may be opportunities that come along that would enhance your skills.

Developing a continuous professional development (CPD) portfolio

A continuous professional development (CPD) portfolio is a file of evidence that you will need to demonstrate your competency. You may be asked by the Health and Care Professions Council to provide this file of evidence at the biennial renewal of your registration; this means your registration and therefore your ability to practise and earn your living will be dependent on the evidence you are able to provide. It is surprising how many students leave the development of a CPD portfolio until the last minute and then realise that it would have been so much better to start it at the beginning of the programme, as the tutors had suggested! You will need this portfolio for the whole of your career, so it is sensible to create a portfolio that is easy to maintain and access.

There are CPD portfolio templates available from a number of sources; your university is likely to provide you with a template or you could access the ePortfolio on the Chartered Society of Physiotherapy's website. If you decide to make your own template, then there are structures you could follow. As an example you may like to use the

National Health Service Knowledge and Skills Framework (Department of Health, 2004). Every physiotherapist has to be able to meet all core dimensions at level 2 and be able to meet the health and wellbeing (HWB) dimensions (HWB6 and HWB7) at level three. You will need to develop a way to cross-reference your evidence, as some evidence will satisfy more than one competency. Whether you do this with letters, numbers or colours is up to you, as long as it is clear and presented in a professional way. Further details on the Knowledge and Skills Framework can be found in Chapter 10.

The evidence you provide to demonstrate your competency should be relevant, contemporaneous and not breach confidentiality. You will need to provide a series of evidence and be able to show that the demonstration of the skill was not just a one-off stroke of luck. So, say you have attended a study day and have been given a certificate that would make a good start, but shouldn't be used as a stand-alone piece of evidence. With it should be the rationale for attending the study day, a reflection on the things that have been learned and an action plan to show how you intend to use the skills in practice. Then to follow this up, a reflection after you have been using the skills for a while, to show how you have progressed, would also add weight to the evidence. You may seek testimonials from peers to supplement your evidence; however, it is useful to ensure the facts are specific rather than a general statement about how nice you are! It is unnecessary to seek to use testimonials from your service users as this could breach their confidentiality. There are so many other effective ways to demonstrate your competency that will not put you at risk of breaking your Professional Code of Conduct.

Top tip

It is not necessary to keep a hard copy (paper-based file) of your evidence. Keeping all your information secure on a computer – remembering to keep a backup of this on a disk, cloud or memory stick – will make it easier to keep the information up to date and tidy. In this way, when you want to create a CPD file of evidence for an interview for example, you can print off specific, crisp, clean documents and put them into a professional file for the occasion. For the hoarders this method also means that you rarely need to actually throw anything out as you can move out of date evidence into a separate file once it is no longer of use.

Final exams

Many programmes have moved away from 'finals', the dreaded final exams at the end of a three-year programme. Within a Master's level programme there may be a formal exam in the form of a *viva voce* element of the dissertation. It is certainly worth checking with individual admissions tutors to clarify this. In order to elicit depth of knowledge at the final stages of training any exam would be likely to be a written piece rather than multiple choice. Some exams are 'seen' in that the student is told the question or choice of questions before the exam in order to prepare. Needless to say, the well-prepared student has nothing to fear.

The National Student Survey and the Postgraduate Taught Experience Survey

During your final year you will be invited to participate in the National Student Survey (NSS) if you have undertaken a BSc (Honours) degree or the Postgraduate Taught Experience Survey if you have undertaken a Postgraduate Diploma or Master's level degree. This is your opportunity to feed back about the whole of the programme you have undertaken. You may have used the results of this feedback from previous students to help to make your application choices and so future students may well value your thoughts and opinions to help them make theirs.

Remember to give feedback about the whole programme, not just the stressful bits. It is essential that you try to keep your emotions from colouring your judgement – try to assess things objectively before submitting something that you regret later. Remember that it is not only students who read the survey; employers do too. If they read negative things about a particular training programme it may put them off employing someone from there. You will have many opportunities to give constructive feedback to your programme team throughout your time on the programme. You will be told how this feedback has been used and why changes are made so you should feel reassured that the team are taking your feedback very seriously.

As the final year progresses you will be able to assess your progress through the marks and feedback you have been given. Don't go it alone or feel you should know all the answers; your personal tutor, the module teams and the programme leader will all still be happy to help you if you are having a difficult time. They understand that students are all different and have different threshold levels to stress – after all, they have all undertaken the physiotherapy training themselves as well as other postgraduate training at Master's and Doctorate level.

Enjoy the opportunities, share your knowledge with other students and celebrate when the final assessment is submitted. It is not the end of the learning process as you will be continuing your professional development throughout your career, but it should be the last formal assignment you have to undertake for a little while at least!

9: What do the final years of studying physiotherapy involve?

Chapter summary

It is surprising just how quickly the final year of your programme will go. Think carefully about the topics for any assignments where you have a choice. You may be able to tailor an assignment to target a key contemporary issue, which may be useful to you later when you are applying for jobs. The final year is an opportunity for you to show how much you have learned and your assignment marks will define your final degree classification – so aim high!

Key points

- Plan your study and relaxation time before you start your final year – and try to stick to it.
- Dissertations or final projects are only hard if you start working on them too late and fail to take advantage of the support offered.
- Don't narrow your skills and experiences in the final year to areas you are interested in at that time. In the future you may need a wider knowledge base.
- Start your CPD file early to reduce unnecessary stress later.
- Don't be afraid of seeking help and support.

Useful resources

Physiotherapy programmes in the UK: www.csp.org.uk

Reference

Agenda for Change Project Team (2004) *The NHS Knowledge and Skills Framework and the Development Review Process.* London, Department of Health.

Chapter 10

What career paths are available to me?

In this chapter we will consider the career paths available to the graduate physiotherapist. Additional information that is crucial to inform your choice of career, such as insurance, mentorship and being part of a professional community, are also discussed. It is never too early to start thinking about the kind of role you would like to have. Try not to limit yourself too early in your training, though, or you may find that you miss out on opportunities. As the contemporary landscape of employment changes, you will need to consider all of the options open to you. The job you want may not be on your doorstep and you may need to revise your plans if you are unable to move readily. Keeping an open mind and being prepared to try different options will make you more flexible within the employment market. First of all we will consider how to get your first job.

Getting your first job

During your final year you will start to think about what you intend to do at the end of your time as a student. All universities have careers advisers who can help you with application forms and practice mock interviews. Some programmes will offer students the opportunity to undertake practice interviews as part of the programme itself and some may have dedicated careers staff assigned to them, which is useful as they should have experience with physiotherapy applications to draw upon.

> 'I was mortified when I realised I was going to have a practice interview! I was so anxious and knew I was wriggling in my seat. After the practice our group sat together and gave each other feedback. I was surprised that people thought some of my answers were good. I used the feedback to help me prepare for the real interview and I was offered the job!'

It may come as a surprise to learn that not all graduates choose to go into physiotherapy straight away. Some will take a gap year to travel and work abroad. Most new graduates take on a post in the National Health Service. Nearly all jobs in these areas are now advertised electronically on sites like Sector 1 and NHS Jobs. You will need to register with these organisations and then, after indicating the types of job, location and pay band, you will get a notification whenever a job is advertised that meets your requirements. You might also like to register with the Chartered Society of Physiotherapy (CSP) Job Escalator – a guide to all things related to gaining employment as a physiotherapist.

You will also find jobs advertised in the *Frontline* magazine. This is a bi-weekly magazine containing news, opinions and upcoming events. This publication is available to members of the CSP as part of the subscription. This may be available in the university library too. Here you may find some highly specialised posts and often advertisements for the different employment agencies that offer locum work.

Locum work may appeal to you, especially if you do not have any dependants or commitments. Locum postings can last from a few days to several months – even years if a post is difficult to fill. You will need to have a degree of flexibility and feel very comfortable in new situations. This kind of work as a first post can be daunting, as you will be expected to function without the usual supervision afforded a new graduate.

Some private healthcare organisations also employ physiotherapists, especially in their special needs units. This can be a challenging area to work in and you may need to arrange your own supervision externally.

You may wish to work in a non-traditional setting – perhaps a charity or school. Many charities advertise posts locally as well as on their websites, so keep checking in the local press for posts. The *Times Educational Supplement* is a useful first port of call for jobs in education (both Local Authority and independent schools). You might have had the opportunity to undertake a role emerging placement in a non-traditional setting and may decide to approach the organisation for a post there, especially if you made a good impression!

There are also now increasing roles for physiotherapists in residential and nursing homes. A significant amount of rehabilitation occurs in these settings and the work can be extremely satisfying. Check the Care Quality Commission (CQC) site for up to date information about any residential or nursing home, as the CQC regularly inspects organisations and can give an objective view. Indeed, you may decide to work for the CQC as either an inspector or as a specialist adviser.

For any job that you apply for you will need to put time aside to complete the application form. All jobs will ask for a personal statement of some sort and it is important to get this right. As so many new graduates will fit the qualifications of the post, it is important you demonstrate that you are the best person for the job through the information on your application form. Take time to read the person specification and respond to the attributes required, indicating how you meet the criteria. Try not to say 'I can do this' or 'I'm good at that' as it really doesn't demonstrate your skills. Give an example of how you meet the criteria to show your competency. Try to emphasise the different contexts and environments you have experienced as an undergraduate eg acute wards, rehabilitation units and community. as this makes the person more immediately employable. The quality of your application form will be the thing that gets you through to an interview. This is then your opportunity to show a panel why they should select you. Again, you should take time to plan for the interview, think about how you might answer the questions and prepare a file of evidence to take with you.

Starting your own business

Starting your own business is also a possibility but requires a lot of enthusiasm and experience as a physiotherapist, as there is less easily accessible, daily professional support. Some business experience would also be very beneficial. This might be your own experience or from a support organisation. There are many independent practitioners working for themselves and undertaking private work. The market for private physiotherapy is potentially lucrative but this is also extremely crowded and hard to gain a foothold as a newcomer. Working for an established private provider may be a better option. This work may be in a specific field, for example insurance work or sports clinics. Most universities have a business unit or entrepreneur centre where business advice can be sought and of course, there is support available through the CSP. You will need to identify the gap in the market and prepare a business case so you can approach a lender for the set-up costs. There are many issues to consider: insurance, work base, security, supervision, marketing and sustainability to name a few. Whether you intend to offer peripatetic sessions to a school or full-time cover to a fitness centre, there are risk factors to balance with the pleasure of determining your own career path. Some of the following information in this chapter will be very important for you to note.

Registering with the Health and Care Professions Council (HCPC)

If you intend to practise as a physiotherapist you will need to apply to register with the Health and Care Professions Council (HCPC). The HCPC is the regulatory body for physiotherapists. As a regulatory body, the HCPC protects the public by keeping a register of all physiotherapists who meet the HCPC standards for training, professional skills, behaviour and health. 'Physiotherapist' is a professional title protected by law. Individuals who are not registered with the HCPC are not allowed to use this title and to do so is classed as a criminal offence. Physiotherapists are required to re-register biannually and may be asked to provide evidence of their continuous professional development in order to fulfil this. If you fail to meet the standards you may be removed from the register, which would mean that you would no longer be able to use the professional title or work as a physiotherapist. It is very important to remember to re-register because if you do not, even if you meet the standards, you may be temporarily unregistered and an employer may suspend you (possibly unpaid) until you are back on the register. This is a costly waste of time and to be avoided.

Top tip

To apply to register you will need to download the application forms from the website, collect the evidence required and get your forms signed by the appropriate people before sending them off with a cheque for the fees. Some employers will not consider your application if you have not already registered, so it is wise to apply as soon as your programme completes so that the forms are waiting at the HCPC ready to be dealt with as soon as your university advises them that you have been successful.

Joining your professional body

The CSP is the professional body for physiotherapists in the UK. This body acts as a trade union, lobbying on your behalf and influencing the direction of the profession in a wide variety of organisations. It is also possible to join the professional body only and not be part of the trade union or to seek union affiliation elsewhere, for example UNISON. The CSP provides a wide range of resources for students and professionals, some of which have been discussed in previous chapters of this book.

Students are encouraged to join the CSP as a student member from the beginning of their programme. Some universities will pay for this while others may not (see also Chapter 6, section Are there professional costs related to my course?). The range of support and learning materials available via the website is ever growing and is invaluable throughout training. As well as this information, the CSP advertises conferences where the professional community gets together to share innovations, research and experiences as part of a shared learning event. It is an opportunity to meet with the researchers and practitioners who are leading the way in physiotherapy practice. As you come to the end of your training programme you will need to consider transferring your membership from that of student member to full professional member.

There are many benefits to being a member of the professional body, all of which are available in their literature and on the website. Just paying your subscription to be a member of the professional body is not enough evidence to demonstrate you are keeping up to date, although it is a start. The organisation itself is member led, which means that it relies upon its members to fully engage in its activities. This could be in the form of joining a local or regional group, attending study events or participating in online discussion forums. You could also join and participate in a specialist section or put yourself forward to become a member of Council. You could be Chair of Council in the future – it is a role open to any upstanding member of the professional community.

Professional indemnity

Professional indemnity insurance is provided through membership of the CSP. This indemnity cover is for claims made against you in the UK and covers negligence, omission and error. At present the indemnity insurance cover is for up to £5 million in any one claim but there are certain exclusions. If you work within a statutory organisation you will automatically be covered by their insurance too. For all other kinds of employment it is advisable that you ask about the insurance arrangements and seek professional advice to ensure that you have the right level of cover. This is where being a part of the professional body is invaluable, as this advice can be sought from the CSP at no cost.

Preceptorship and mentorship

Starting your first job can be stressful, whether you are in a large and busy department or working independently. Many organisations now offer a system of preceptorship for new graduates to help to support them through the first six months of their new role. Each organisation will have different guidelines, but the principles are similar.

Mentorship is when you select someone to support you through a period of your career. It is unlikely to be your employer or line manager; rather it should be someone with relevant experience who is at a distance from your working environment. Their role is to facilitate your thinking and decision-making by asking you sensible and relevant questions to help you to work out the best course of action. They should give you honest feedback. A mentor who always agrees with everything you say is not being truthful to the process. Equally, a mentor who only points out the negatives could seriously undermine your confidence. It is important to establish some ground rules with your mentor. Decide how long this relationship will last and the specific goals you wish to achieve. Take time to evaluate the process so you keep on track. You should choose a different mentor for the different situations you encounter and want to develop in, to ensure you have the right person supporting you. This is often a good topic to discuss in an interview.

The NHS Knowledge and Skills Framework (KSF)

The NHS Knowledge and Skills Framework (KSF) (Department of Health, 2004) was developed to provide a specific framework of the knowledge and skills required by all of the different staff (except dentists and doctors) who work within the NHS. It defines and describes the skills in a consistent way and it will be used (if you work in the NHS) to review your development and progress. It should support the direction of your continuous professional development (CPD) and can be used to form the framework for your CPD file of competencies.

It is wise to take time to understand the framework as it is a very useful structure to help describe the acquisition and development of your knowledge and skills. You show how you use your knowledge in practice, how you have developed to be able to undertake more complex interventions and how you have put your postgraduate training into practice. It is very important that you are able to show that you are keeping your skills up to date. Quality services depend on the staff within them maintaining their competencies – after all, you wouldn't want to be treated by someone who hadn't bothered to keep up to date.

Whether you work in the NHS or not, this is a very useful tool. You can download a copy from the Department of Health website.

Choosing a speciality

Many students arrive at the physiotherapy programme with an idea of which area they would like to work in when they eventually qualify. Others may have been seconded by their employer to undertake their training. If this is the case for you, you may be returning to a particular area of work and may need to fulfil a contractual obligation before making your first career choices. One thing is for sure; during the programme you will have been given the opportunity to experience physiotherapy in a number of practice placement settings and also through theoretical study within the university. Your ideas may have changed and you will need to evaluate the kind of jobs you will be looking for.

One opportunity that may be available to you is a rotational post. A rotational post is when an employer offers a job that allows you to work in several different physiotherapy services in turn. Each rotation usually lasts between four and six months. These rotations may be in only one sector or you may be offered mixed rotations that are in both acute and community settings – there are many different possibilities. A rotational post allows you to try different areas of practice before deciding on the area you want to specialise in.

Specialising doesn't happen straight away. You can expect to be in a graduate post for up to two years in order to begin to feel really confident in your skills. It is advisable not to move up the professional grades too quickly, as this tends to prevent you from really learning the competencies to gain a solid base from which to practise.

Becoming a consultant physiotherapist

There are opportunities for physiotherapists who become specialised in a particular area to apply for a consultant post. These posts were developed to enable practitioners to have a senior clinical and leadership role. As well as delivering expert clinical practice, you will be expected to undertake some teaching in this role and would certainly be expected to undertake research audit and the evaluation of treatment and services. It is a great opportunity to be a key leader and influencer in strategic and service changes. Your research will create the evidence base that will improve services.

Taking the management path

Becoming a manager is a rewarding and challenging role. There are management roles within large and small teams, and you may feel that you have the skills to manage a service in an efficient and effective way. You will need to have developed excellent leadership skills in order to undertake these management roles well. If you enjoy personnel management, budgeting, planning and evaluation then this is the challenge for you. You may find yourself managing your own business or managing a diverse team within one of the statutory services. Being a leader in this way isn't for everyone and can divert you away from working directly with service users, but the opportunity to ensure services are as good as they can be is equally satisfying. A role in management is often taken following additional postgraduate studies in leadership or management and these will help you develop your skills and enhance your understanding of the theories and practicalities of leadership.

During your training you will have ample opportunity to read and discuss other people's research. Creating the research evidence on which best practice is based is an essential role within the profession.

If you are able to attend conferences you will be able to listen to presentations about the research that has been carried out – it is an inspirational experience! Depending on the programme you study, you may have the opportunity to undertake your own small-scale research, be involved in others' research or develop an extended research proposal. You will understand the types of research that can be undertaken, how to interpret the outcomes and how to use this to shape the interventions you use every day in your practice.

Case study: Becoming a researcher – Cormac Ryan

During my final six months of training to become a physiotherapist I undertook a research project investigating muscle activity around the knee joint. It was during this period that I realised how much I enjoyed the research process and considered research as a career path. I discussed this with my lecturers who were very positive about research as a career and unanimously highlighted the importance of undertaking a PhD should I choose a research path. However, I received two different recommendations about how to go about it. Some recommended I undertake at least two years of clinical practice prior to embarking upon a PhD so as to embed my new skills as a clinical physiotherapist and to gain important clinical experience that would inform my future research. Others recommended that I go directly into a PhD as often once an individual starts working it is very difficult to give up a well-paid enjoyable job to become a student once again, and this can become a barrier to undertaking the PhD at all. In the end, I found a middle ground; I undertook a full-time PhD immediately upon completing my training but simultaneously I worked in a busy NHS outpatient department two mornings every week for three years. This gave me the best of both worlds. I now work as a full-time researcher in a UK university investigating how to best help patients manage conditions such as low back pain. Ultimately, my goal is to undertake research that will improve frontline clinical practice and thus potentially help in the rehabilitation of literally millions of people worldwide.

It is essential that all physiotherapists contribute in some way towards creating the body of evidence required for the profession. You may decide to look for a research post, usually based in a university research department or teaching hospital. Here you will get the opportunity to undertake your own research and get paid to do so. Another way to undertake research is via further academic study – moving on to a Master's level programme and a Doctorate (PhD). Usually you undertake these kinds of study at the same time as working – which has its positive and negative aspects. Some PhD students are full-time students who are paid. Again, there is a wide range of ways to undertake further study, so you should look around to see what suits you best.

Thinking about teaching

All physiotherapists need to be trained and teaching is another way to help to share your skills in order to help others achieve their goals. As a practitioner you should get the opportunity to participate in students' practice placements – either for one-off activities or as their placement educator. As a specialist you may be invited to give special lectures within the physiotherapy programme too. Once you have had the chance to try out your teaching skills you may consider a teaching post. Most lecturer posts require you to have studied a Master's degree. Some universities will sponsor you to undertake a Master's as part of the conditions of your employment. You will also need to undertake and pass a Postgraduate Certificate in Learning and Teaching in Higher Education (PGCLTHE), or similar.

Case study: Becoming a lecturer – David Grover

I decided to move into higher education after 13 years working in clinical practice for the NHS because I enjoyed working alongside students on clinical placement and had received generally positive feedback about my own performance in that role. I also had the opportunity to deliver some informal teaching in the UK and Russia (in English!) and thoroughly enjoyed both experiences.

When a physiotherapy teaching post at Teesside University presented itself I applied for it successfully. I was fortunate to be able to obtain this job without any formal teaching qualifications. When I started working at the university, I was contractually obliged to work towards a PGCE qualification and subsequently a full Master's, both of which I've now completed. I would say I was lucky to be able to make a career change in this way because studying for such qualifications whilst working full time clinically would have been extremely challenging and I guess I'll never know if I would have stayed the course with that. When I started working in higher education I actually found delivering teaching sessions and imparting

> knowledge and experience relatively straightforward because initially I was covering material very much within my comfort zone and in effect talking to students about my previous employment. More challenging by far was the academic side of the role, such as understanding assessment criteria, teaching to defined learning outcomes, designing modules and mentoring students effectively through dissertations and other work. These took me several years to become confident and competent and I can't emphasise enough how useful my own Master's qualification is in helping me fulfil this role.

Teaching the next generation of physiotherapists is a great responsibility, shared between the university teaching staff and the practice educators. University teaching staff do not enjoy the same lengthy holidays that the students have – work goes on throughout the year, even if all of your friends presume you will be having a lazy time during the summer!

Working internationally

If you plan to work overseas you may need to start the application process almost as soon as you start your final year. To work in some countries you will need a Master's degree, so if you have studied a BSc (Hons) programme you will need to complete a fast track Master's programme before you can apply. You will be able to find out which universities offer this kind of programme from the CSP website. There are plenty of overseas recruitment agencies that will be looking to sign you up. They each offer different packages, so it is worthwhile attending their publicity days to find out more before you sign any contracts. Some countries will require you to undertake additional examinations in order to register to work there. Going through an agency will make it easier to find this out; however, you can contact the specific Health Board for the country you would like to work in to get the up to date information you need.

If you are planning to work in the Republic of Ireland there is a complex application process to undertake. Your personal tutor and placement tutor will need to provide a variety of evidence too, so it is advisable to discuss your application with them before you complete your final year. Further information on international perspectives is included in Chapter 13.

Chapter summary

As a physiotherapist there are so many opportunities available to you that you may have difficulty deciding on your career path! While some people will concentrate on getting a job and making short-term plans, others may have a long-term career pathway in mind that requires careful planning. Whatever you plan to do, make sure you keep your programme leader or personal tutor informed when you get your first job, as this is important information they will need. Your tutors will be interested to hear about your progress over the years too and you may find yourself being asked back to share your experiences.

Key points

- Submit your application for the Health and Care Professions Council register as soon as you complete your programme and remember to re-register every two years.

- Discuss your employment plans with your personal tutor – they may be responsible for writing your reference so they need to know all about you.

- Plan your future direction of study so that you have the correct level of degree for the career of your choice.

- Join your professional body and be an active member – this will offer you support and enhance your continuous professional development.

Useful resources

Sector 1: http://sector1.net/

NHS Jobs: www.jobs.nhs.uk

Chartered Society of Physiotherapy jobs: www.jobescalator.com

Reference

Agenda for Change Project Team (2004) *The NHS Knowledge and Skills Framework and the Development Review Process.* London, Department of Health.

Chapter 11

Physiotherapy in the statutory sector

In this chapter we will consider the work undertaken by physiotherapists who work within the National Health Service (NHS). A smaller number of physiotherapists work within the local authority (social care). Many changes have been made to the statutory services in the recent past. Successive governments across the political spectrum have required these services to modernise, streamline and increase the level of quality. It has been a long process, with many staff feeling the constant pressure of change. Despite the changes, physiotherapists are still leading innovative practice in the sector and it is unlikely that physiotherapists would not have a role in these areas in the future.

The National Health Service (NHS)

The NHS has many different services where physiotherapists can be found. Acute and foundation hospitals provide essential care for people who need emergency care or who have planned medical interventions. Physiotherapists can be found right at the heart of emergency care, working in the Accident and Emergency (A&E) department assessing individuals to see if it is possible to avoid a hospital admission. Physiotherapists work on the medical, surgical, orthopaedic and mental health wards, in paediatrics, hand clinics, wheelchair services, stroke teams, burns and plastic surgery and long-term conditions. They are also heavily involved in intermediate care and other community-based teams. Intermediate care is a service where, as well as trying to prevent unnecessary admissions, the physiotherapists work to speed up the discharges. Physiotherapists are also involved in end of life care, working in palliative care and on regional teams for illnesses such as HIV and AIDS.

There are so many different areas where physiotherapists are employed within the NHS. Most often there is a physiotherapy department, with assessment and treatment facilities and office space. This is used as a base and the physiotherapists will often see their service users on the wards, only bringing them to the department for specific interventions. In other areas physiotherapists work within inter-professional teams. This is when a group of different professionals work in a team, generally with a specific service user group – for example an intermediate care team – working from a shared base. Some teams are a mixture of NHS staff and social services staff, who work together to ensure the best service for their service users. An example of joint working in this way is a learning disability team.

The NHS provides free care at the point of need. Physiotherapists will nevertheless become involved in assessing needs and making recommendations with regard to mobility equipment provision. As well as assessing and treating the service users, reports need to be written, records kept and liaison with other members of the inter-professional team maintained. These other activities can take up considerable time and are an essential part of the role. Physiotherapists are regularly assisted by physiotherapy assistants, technical instructors or generic assistants. The physiotherapist must learn how to prioritise their work and delegate specific tasks to other members of the team. In addition to the assessments and treatment interventions that are undertaken within the hospital, physiotherapists may attend home assessments with an occupational therapist in the service user's home, to check the service user's safety and independence.

The following case studies aim to give some insight into a selection of physiotherapy roles in the NHS. Unfortunately there is not enough space in an introductory book like this to include every kind of team or service in detail – hopefully those that have been chosen will help you to put physiotherapy into perspective. In addition, we have included some longer examples of a day in the life of some physiotherapists in the final chapter of this book. As a physiotherapist you will have a variety of different roles to fulfil regardless of the setting in which you work. These examples will give a flavour of that variety and the tasks to be completed.

Case study: Working as an inpatient rotational physiotherapist – Katie Halford

It all started four years ago: a newly qualified physiotherapist eager for a job in the NHS. I was drawn to the NHS by my drive to work in the public sector and an eagerness to gain a variety of skills and experiences in different specialist roles. With my degree and my resolve to work in the NHS, I was soon appointed as a band 5 rotational physiotherapist after a brief period as a locum physiotherapy assistant.

I first began working in spinal injuries rehabilitation, treating patients with spinal cord injuries within the acute setting, utilising my respiratory, neurological and musculoskeletal knowledge. I worked closely within a multidisciplinary team to address all the service users' needs by attending family/best interest meetings, completing joint assessments and delivering a holistic treatment plan. After six months of gaining the knowledge and confidence in this specialist area I rotated to face a new challenge.

The daunting task of starting a new rotation soon diminished when I realised the invaluable experience I would gain. With more ease I drew upon my knowledge from each specialism to tailor my assessments and treatments to that area. I received monthly supervisions and in-service training from senior staff and was encouraged to discuss any problems that may arise. This in turn allowed me to become a well-rounded professional, who could draw upon skills and strengths from a variety of settings to deliver a high-quality service.

After six months, I was provided further respiratory training in a number of areas to enable me to work on the on-call respiratory rota. I was allocated weekend shifts and evening on-call shifts, in which I covered the physiotherapy respiratory service. I was supported on the weekends with another physiotherapist and in the evenings I had a 'buddy' who was an assigned senior physiotherapist who could be contacted in an emergency. The challenge of working on the respiratory rota strengthened my autonomy and cemented my knowledge and confidence in that area.

Approaching my third year of work within the NHS, I was successful in being promoted to a band 6 inpatient rotational physiotherapist. New challenges arose as I had more responsibilities to assist in managing a physiotherapy team, supporting junior staff, providing service improvement and training. Conversely, as a band 6 I worked within each specialism for 9 months instead of 6 months which enabled more time to establish a unified, cohesive and well-trained team.

In summary, the strength of working as a rotational physiotherapist within the NHS challenged me to work in a variety of areas drawing upon transferable skills and experiences. The nature of a rotational member of staff meant that there was a constant change in environment and staff which, mixed with a busy and challenging environment, heightened individual and team anxiety. However, by working within different team dynamics and approaches, I learnt strategies to overcome pressures to provide the highest quality of care. Moreover, by working with highly skilled senior staff there was always an endless opportunity to develop my professional development and feel supported in every decision. In my opinion, the opportunity to be a rotational NHS physiotherapist should be sought, as it enables you to experience all areas and specialise in your chosen area and allows you to develop within a supportive environment.

Becoming a Physiotherapist

Case study: Working as a community physiotherapist – Fiona Hartley, Highly Specialised/Team Leader Physiotherapist

I am a Community Physiotherapist, working in rural Scotland. My area covers towns, villages, farms and the beautiful Scottish countryside and glens. I am based in a small hospital and oversee the care of the elderly rehabilitation ward located there, but the majority of my work is in the community. I see people in their own homes, which could also be sheltered housing or care homes, or at day care centres. I see anyone over the age of 16, though the majority of people are over 65. There are various schemes (early supported discharge, prevention of admission, enhanced community support, enablement) but ultimately I aim to provide physiotherapy to anyone who requires it in their own home, to maintain and improve their functional independence.

I see a broad range of conditions and problems including:

- Orthopaedic – joint replacements, fractures
- Neurological – stroke, multiple sclerosis, Parkinson's disease, motor neurone disease
- Musculoskeletal – back, neck or joint pain, osteoarthritis, rheumatoid arthritis
- Respiratory – chest infection, chronic obstructive pulmonary disease, pulmonary fibrosis
- Palliative care
- Mobility problems, balance problems, falls

I provide classes in the area for Better Balance, Pulmonary Rehabilitation and Cardiac Rehabilitation. I work very closely with the other members of the multidisciplinary team. I have weekly meetings at the GP practice, with colleagues from healthcare and social work, along with carers' support and voluntary services.

One of the best things about working in the community is really getting to know the people that you see regularly. If they need to come into hospital, you know all about their home situation, support network and care package. This can facilitate a much quicker and safer discharge home. You build a trust and mutual respect with them which can only enhance their care. Every day is different and varied and although it can be very busy, I thoroughly enjoy it.

Case study: Working in the NHS – David Alderson, Senior Physiotherapist

As a senior physiotherapist within musculoskeletal services in the NHS, I'm required to maintain a busy caseload of referrals from both GP, orthopaedic, rheumatology and other specialist sources. This means diverse patient groups of all ages are managed within our service. Geographically, the 200,000 population is spread over a very large area and as a result, therapies are delivered in small community hospitals, GP practices and health centres in addition to the main hospital hub. A flexible approach is very important with this in mind, as demand can change based on a number of different factors.

A typical day sees a physiotherapist at my grade assess and treat 15+ patients per day, a combination of new patients and reviews. The diary is managed autonomously and thankfully there is some administrative support, but we book our own reviews. Within a working week, a physiotherapist may be in two to three different locations, delivering exercise programmes in a gym or providing education for persistent problems. Communication is often required with the upper and lower limb and spinal physiotherapy specialities and is in addition to frequent contact with GPs and orthopaedic services locally.

All services are under pressure these days and we strive for greater efficiency through approaches such as gym-based classes or groups, development of treatment pathways or self-referral and physiodirect consultations. Physiodirect consultations are done both face to face and over the phone and serve to allow an assessment of whether formal physiotherapy input is needed, onwards referral required or just education, advice and discharge. Further service developments are made through auditing outcome measures and patient flow (including Did Not Attend and Unable to Attend rates) and there are always additional projects being driven by our senior physiotherapists around paperwork and individual therapist management approaches. Additional challenges within physiotherapy include support of junior staff and students and ensuring good-quality education and staff support is provided. It is also essential to maintain your own knowledge through self-directed reading and a monthly in-house training programme is delivered by all members of the team. As a profession we are seeing physiotherapy evolve and in musculoskeletal care physiotherapists are appearing in different settings. These include advanced practitioner posts in GP practices or A&E departments for example. Exciting times lie ahead in physiotherapy!

Inter-professional working

All professionals working with service users are encouraged to work inter-professionally. This means that they come together sharing their skills and expertise to ensure that the best possible plan of interventions is made for each individual service user. Throughout your training to become a physiotherapist you will be encouraged to find out about the other professions that physiotherapists work alongside. Both in training and once you are in practice you will get the opportunity to work with such professionals and develop your skills together. It is important to understand the different roles and value each other's contribution to good service delivery.

Chapter summary

There are so many different opportunities in the statutory sector, which is traditionally where physiotherapists have been employed. Although there have been major changes to the contemporary landscape of the National Health Service and social care, there is still a requirement for physiotherapy. You may find yourself involved with service improvement initiatives or setting up new services, which is very exciting. The physiotherapists who have shared their experiences in this book have had careers of varying lengths; however, their energy and enthusiasm for the work they do is still as high as it was when they first qualified. They continue to be inspirational.

Key points

- Statutory services provide a wide variety of opportunities for physiotherapists.
- Often there will be a significant number of physiotherapists working in larger organisations so there is a professional community for support.

Useful resources

The Chartered Society of Physiotherapy: www.csp.org.uk

Chapter 12

Physiotherapy in the non-statutory sector

12: Physiotherapy in the non-statutory sector

The opportunities for physiotherapists to work outside the statutory sector in private practice are vast. This chapter will briefly consider some of these areas and offer insight and experience to help you consider future career opportunities.

When you have gained a degree of experience and feel that you would like to work for yourself there is the possibility of functioning as a private practitioner. This will make a whole new set of demands of you which may not have been included in detail in your initial training as a physiotherapist and so the decision should not be taken lightly. You will not only have to maintain records of your client contacts but also the records of your business. This will require you to develop a new set of IT skills. This will involve the use of databases and spreadsheets as you will be required to set up your own accounts and manage your own caseload and business contacts. You may need to develop your business planning skills. It will be necessary to seek funding for your work, seek out suppliers and develop less expensive strategies for interventions which will be more efficient. You may even feel like diversifying to add additional services to your business portfolio, such as offering health promotion activities. This role will allow you to see the strengths and limitations of working in the statutory sector. You can determine which clients you want to work with and how you want to develop your professional skills. Whilst there are many advantages to this role, you will also need to recognise the changes required. There will be no sick pay or pension rights and you will have to consider this separately. You may also become responsible for paying others for working for you, which will bring other considerations. There are no guarantees in private practice but there are a great many opportunities that many find particularly rewarding.

This chapter will briefly consider some of these areas and offer insight and experience to help you consider future career opportunities.

Case study: Private practice – Kate Bye, Co-Director and Senior Physiotherapist, North Yorkshire Physiotherapy

Private practice comes in all shapes and sizes. I work in a small independent clinic that I established with fellow physio, Dallas Newton, in 2013. Having only had a few forays into the private sector in various settings whilst working in the NHS, this was a huge challenge to me but one I have loved.

Word is spreading to the general public about the benefits physiotherapy can provide and many people now have private health insurance or are willing to pay for their treatment if they are unable to wait for, or travel to, NHS appointments. Although the majority of my clients are musculoskeletal based, we also have specialists in neurological and Women's Health physiotherapy.

Our clients are ever varied, ranging from acute to long standing, single joint to multiple trauma, pre-operative to post-operative and respiratory problems to balance and mobility issues. Having had a wide variety of experience and teachings in the NHS I feel very prepared to deal with many conditions that may come through the door, as well as the occasional non-physio presentation that needs dealing with in a different way.

One of the enjoyable aspects of working in private practice is dealing with highly motivated individuals who want to return to as full a function as they possibly can. They generally respond well to being educated to manage their condition with guidance from us. We have the privilege of being able to treat as we feel best for the client and being able to maximise their recovery with options for gait analysis in the clinic, cross-referrals and a network of other health and exercise professionals we can link in with. The satisfaction at seeing a client delighted in their abilities to do something they didn't think possible is indescribable.

The environments in which we work stretch beyond the treatment room. We have successful physio-led back exercise classes and balance classes for the elderly and we provide home or nursing home visits. We also attend a local business providing advice on general aches, pains and injuries, helping staff with their working practices enhancing productivity and job satisfaction.

Our passion for physiotherapy takes us into situations where we can showcase our profession. We have provided many presentations and training, hosted stands, been interviewed for books and newspaper articles and I've even been on local radio! These are fantastic opportunities to raise the profile of the profession in an increasingly competitive market, demonstrating the range of skills we have. As physios, we believe we are best placed to fully rehabilitate clients, promote self-management and empower individuals to care for their own health and wellbeing and we are committed to getting this message across to the general public.

Private physiotherapy has wonderful benefits but also its own sets of challenges, mainly dealing with health insurance companies and intermediaries. Physio First are working with private practitioners collecting and analysing data to prove to insurance companies the value of physiotherapy, not only to individuals but also to society and the economy as a whole.

> I love working in the independent sector but I believe that as long as you love your profession, you can thrive wherever you like.

Alternatively you might like to work in or alongside a charity. As well as the many nationally recognised charities, there are opportunities to work in specialised areas with smaller charities. The following case study shows how physiotherapists are making an impact with seafarers.

Case study: Charitable sector – Claire Petersen, Harbourside Physiotherapy Team working with the Seafarers Hospital Society

Harbourside Physiotherapy located in Newlyn, West Cornwall, serves a community centred around one of the largest fishing ports in the UK. The local mining, farming and fishing community has suffered major hardships over recent times, but fishing has continued to be a major employer in the community, and remains one of the most dangerous and physically demanding jobs in the UK.

This unique environment and the specific needs of the fishing industry have seen the practice privileged to partner with the Seafarers Hospital Society (SHS) charity, as a Musculoskeletal and Occupational Health primary contact, and innovating physiotherapy services and delivery – specifically tailored to the needs and demands of fishermen and those working at sea.

The SHS supported a pilot study led by Harbourside, working with the local community of fishermen, who found it difficult to access physiotherapy through standard NHS services, and who were consequently often at sea working with either injuries and pain or long-term physical problems. The SHS supports the health of all seafarers, whether merchant seafarers or fishermen, in part in association with the Dreadnought Medical Service in London – but responded to the specific Cornwall fishing community needs enabling fishermen to access immediate physiotherapy with flexible appointments and treatment from therapists with industry knowledge and understanding of the working conditions faced at sea. The initial SHS/Harbourside project undertaken in Newlyn provided information on the health and wellbeing of fishermen and seafarers, allowing a better understanding of their work and encouraging preventative pathways and participatory ergonomics to play a leading role in supporting a healthier work life for those in the Newlyn commercial fishing fleet.

After successful trials with Newlyn fishermen, this programme is now being extended to provide similar access for other fishing and seafaring communities throughout the UK.

Working for a professional team might be where your ambitions lie. This case study shows the dedication and hard work required when working for a professional football team.

Case study: Sports physiotherapy (football) – David Annison, Senior Specialist Physiotherapist

Once qualified and registered as a physiotherapist there are many paths the profession can take you down. I was fortunate enough to work at the top level of English football within a Premier League football club. My path into football started with hours of voluntary work with local rugby clubs whilst also developing within an NHS musculoskeletal role. It was during my voluntary work that I was asked to take a lead role the following season with a semi-professional rugby league team. From this opportunity came further experiences such as European pre-season training camps and working for the Women's RFL England squad to televised Super League and international games. With the knowledge and skills I developed I was appointed into the medical team of a Premier League football team and continued there for many seasons.

A typical day for a sports physiotherapist generally starts with a large medical team meeting whereby players are discussed in terms of the current status of their rehabilitation programme. The team meeting often includes the sports science department, sports therapists, and strength and conditioning specialists as well as the team doctor and psychologist. The player is then discussed from a holistic viewpoint and, depending on their greatest need, will be directed to the most suitable professional to be managed for that stage of their care.

From a physiotherapist viewpoint, the spectrum of care can be wide and varied. This ranges from those who have undergone surgical intervention, and managed strictly, to those players ready to return to the field of play. In the early stages of rehabilitation a physiotherapist will work closely with all departments to ensure a plan is created to deliver the best outcome of an injured area whilst maintaining global cardiovascular fitness and strength. Specific and progressive training regimes are then designed and followed closely to ensure that the area of injury undergoes loading to improve symptoms, but not significant enough to overload them. The medical team will then discuss the outcome data of a return to play fitness test designed to recreate the rigors of competition. Utilising GPS and video technology, as well as clinical information, a decision is made as to

12: Physiotherapy in the non-statutory sector

whether a player is both safe enough and fit enough to return to training. This process is generally phased and will often see players training in controlled environments for several weeks prior to their return to competition.

Physiotherapy delivered in a sporting environment is not generally restricted to a clinic basis. As injured player numbers tend to be lower than in healthcare environments, more time is available to ensure that a detailed assessment and effective treatment is delivered to each player's needs. Treatments can include massage, stretching, strengthening and electrotherapy treatments. In elite environments the use of specialised equipment such as hydrotherapy pools, specialised muscle stimulators and anti-gravity treadmills are also available to use.

A publicised role of the physiotherapist is the musculoskeletal medical examination carried out prior to a player signing a contract with a professional club. This medical aims to highlight any major injury history and if any problems remain which may pose future problems when the player is signed into a new contract. Medicals are now routinely carried out for all signed players of all age groups in order to identify areas of development or pre-habilitation. This ensures any musculoskeletal problem identified early can be improved upon which may reduce the risk of future injury to the player. The physiotherapist plays a key role in this area and is likely to continue to work long term with a player to ensure they remain as low risk to injury as possible.

Away from the training ground a physiotherapist's role is to ensure player health and safety whilst travelling with the squad and on the pitch. Pre-match strappings and stretching regimes are carried out, as well as any specific pre-game drills that need to be completed. Once a game is underway the physiotherapist remains vigilant to observe for any injuries sustained to players and can enter the field of play should the player require medical assistance. Players can then be screened on the pitch for major injuries and receive treatment should they require it, or removed from the field should they be unable to continue.

The most rewarding aspect of a sports physiotherapist role is to see a player return to competition after months of hard work in rehabilitation. The rehabilitation process for some players can be a long journey therefore a physiotherapist needs to be innovative with their thinking as well as a good listener! Although demanding and often challenging, a role in sports physiotherapy is extremely rewarding and develops a high level of understanding in functional movement and exercise therapy.

New areas of independent practice

One increasingly popular area for independent practice has come in response to the Government's welfare reform agenda and attitudes to Personal Independence Payments. This has resulted in a great number of individuals being assessed to determine the amount of funding they might receive in order to help with the extra costs caused by a disability or long-term ill-health. As this payment is determined by the way a condition affects the individual engaging in activities of daily living rather than the condition itself, this means that everyone must be considered independently. This will require you, as a therapist, to assess the individual and complete a legal report which will support the claimant through their benefit journey. This may require you to work evenings and weekends as this meets the circumstances of the client group.

The Chartered Society of Physiotherapy website has a whole host of further examples where physiotherapists are leading the way into unchartered areas of practice. Their strong message is not to allow yourself to become pigeonholed but to create opportunities and influence change.

Chapter summary

While this area of practice offers a range of differences to the statutory sector, the role of the physiotherapist remains very similar. The intervention process remains the same and the therapist will draw upon the same skills as well as developing a new set of skills around managing or adapting to a different model of relating to the client group. While the case studies in this chapter have offered some examples of physiotherapy practice, they barely scratch the surface of what therapists might achieve. The following chapter will consider the international perspective of physiotherapy.

Key points

- The possibilities are endless in this sector.
- Advice about business and financial issues will be essential.

Useful resources

The Organisation of Chartered Physiotherapists in Private Practice (Physio First): www.csp.org.uk/tagged/organisation-chartered-physiotherapists-private-practice-physio-first

Chapter 13

International perspectives

The World Confederation for Physical Therapy represents physiotherapists globally (www.wcpt.org). Their website contains lots of useful information to assist with your education and training and serves as a very valuable resource for your continuous professional development if you were to decide to work abroad.

Strong international links help the profession to better support the changing demands of a worldwide population. It is not uncommon for international students to come to the UK to study. This might be enrolling on one of the courses already mentioned in Chapter 3 or it might be about updating or enhancing previous studies. For some this is completing additional work to top up a Diploma in Physiotherapy or completing studies at Master's level in order to seek opportunities more easily in the international job market.

As a student, there are often opportunities to engage with students from other countries. The Erasmus+ programme supports education and training with organisations that seek to enhance the learning experience of their students. Erasmus+ can provide funding to allow participants to pursue stimulating learning opportunities across Europe. This may mean that there are opportunities to study elsewhere in Europe and learn on the programmes of partner universities. This will help you to develop your transferable skills. There will be increased opportunities not only to develop your international view of physiotherapy but also to appreciate the cultural differences which might exist across Europe. This might be something you can discuss at interview or once you have commenced your programme of studies.

For many, there is an interest in working overseas. The countries which are most often considered are the US, Canada, Australia and New Zealand. Having your degree in physiotherapy will not always be enough for this transition. Some countries require different registration requirements which new graduates need to be made aware of, so if you are thinking of working abroad after qualification you should make detailed enquiries about the specific country via their professional body. If you are studying overseas and are considering working in the UK, the Chartered Society of Physiotherapy has very useful information available via their website.

Top tips

- Use the information from the World Confederation for Physical Therapy website to help you if you are considering working abroad.
- Always check with local professional bodies to ensure you understand any educational or practice requirements that are required for the country you plan to work in.

The following case studies give an insight into what motivated two different physiotherapists to venture abroad to work and the benefits they felt they gained from this experience.

Case study: Becoming a physiotherapist in the international environment – Brigitte Fiechter Lienert

I was motivated to become a physiotherapist because I wanted to work with people, learn about their biographies and lifestyles, and understand the link between these and their medical problems. A further motivating factor was my interest in movement, the expressiveness of the body, and the physiological connections which, as a physiotherapist, you can influence.

I had had a fascination with other cultures for quite some time, but couldn't see how I could combine this interest with my future profession. Fortunately, during the first semester of my studies, I had a lecturer who critically related his experiences as a doctor. His remarks further awoke my curiosity and convinced me that my future lay in working as a physiotherapist in an international project. His reflections also made me aware of my concern for and sensitivity to others, and I listened to him gladly. Following this incident many years passed because, in those days, an international semester wasn't possible and following graduation I also needed to gain work experience. Many Non-Governmental Organisations demand the requisite professional experience and personal skills in order to work with people in other cultural contexts. I used this period to work on short medical projects of a few weeks each in various parts of the world. Important to me was always to reflect on my relationship to others and my activities, the improvement in medical and physiotherapeutic knowledge, and also to understand the relationship of people to their bodies and movement, which is culturally shaped.

The experiences gained during these assignments benefited me for a long time and are still essential to my activities in Switzerland today, because cultural differences and sensitivities are also important in Swiss physiotherapeutic practice.

There followed a longer assignment as a physiotherapist in Rwanda, a land that has been dominated by war and injury. After this experience, I was convinced that I had to continue my work with the physiotherapeutic treatment of war and torture victims in Switzerland. For many years, I was involved with an inter-disciplinary team in an outpatient clinic for war and torture victims. These assignments and experiences continue to accompany me today in my practical activities, as well as in my teaching as a lecturer at the Zurich University of Applied Sciences.

I am convinced that trainee physiotherapists should be made aware of and prepared for these issues. Internships abroad both during and after their studies should be employed critically and according to expertise. As a physiotherapist I am committed to this aim in both my practical and academic activities.

Becoming a physiotherapist is a first step to combining exploration of the world in all its aspects and empowering people in need.

This final case study explains the route to becoming a physiotherapist in Malaysia and the opportunities available there.

Case study: Perspectives of a Malaysian physiotherapist – Rajkumar Krishnan Vasanthi, Head of Department of Wellness & Physiotherapy, Kuala Lumpur Metropolitan University College

Malaysia is a booming industrialised market economy among the Association of South-East Asian Nation (ASEAN) countries with a total estimated population at 31.7 million in 2016. The average life expectancy at birth is expected to be 74.7 years in 2016 which has continued to rise over the past decades.

In order to create an effective, efficient, fair and high-tech system of healthcare in Malaysia, the '1 Care for 1 Malaysia' plan plays a vital role. Like any other healthcare professionals in Malaysia, physiotherapists play a major role in treating patients with a wide range of impairments. Currently to practise as a physiotherapist the minimum requirement is completion of a formal diploma in physiotherapy with a minimum 1,000 hours of clinical training throughout the educational programme. Any student who has graduated as a physiotherapist is eligible to carry out the practice privately or with a healthcare team in various private or government hospitals or rehabilitation centres. These can be in urban or extremely rural areas. There are growing numbers of physiotherapists working within industry, providing specialist health promotion advice as well as offering treatment directly to employees. Malaysian physiotherapists can opt to be a member of the Malaysian Physiotherapy Association (MPA), a professional body representing Malaysian Physiotherapists, and also a member of the World Confederation for Physical Therapy (WCPT).

Moving forward, the Malaysian Ministry of Health – Allied Health Sciences Division has gazetted the Allied Health Professions Act 2016 (AHPA) which provides the establishment of the Malaysian Allied Health Professions Council. Since physiotherapists are listed as Allied Health Professionals in Malaysia, it is mandatory to register under this council and avail a practising certificate/temporary practising certificate to practise as a physiotherapist in the near future. Malaysian physiotherapists must adhere to the AHPA 2016 code of practice. So, as an essential professional in the healthcare delivery system, Malaysian physiotherapists are caring, committed and competent in providing appropriate healthcare to all.

13: International perspectives

Chapter summary

The international focus within physiotherapy programmes may vary; however, you can be assured that the Chartered Society of Physiotherapy is committed to working with its European and worldwide colleagues to ensure that physiotherapy is used to its full potential to help individuals. The world feels a smaller place with the increase in technology and improvement in available low cost transport. You can play an active part in providing physiotherapy in both developed and developing countries, sharing good practice and bringing home new ideas.

Key points

- There are many organisations which offer long- and short-term placements in a wide variety of countries.
- Positions are available for paid employment and voluntary work.
- Some countries will require you to take further examinations or to have a Master's degree.

Useful resources

Department of Health (2010) *The Framework for NHS Involvement in International Development.* London, Crown.

Voluntary Services Overseas: www.vso.org.uk/volunteer

Outreach International: www.outreachinternational.co.uk

Chapter 14

A day in the life – physiotherapy in action

14: A day in the life – physiotherapy in action

In this chapter we have provided six examples provided by highly skilled physiotherapists working in different areas of practice. Nothing can replace spending time shadowing a physiotherapist, which would allow you the opportunity to ask questions – but hopefully these case studies will provide you with an insight, enabling you to finalise your career choice. There is also a snapshot into a typical day at university, so that you can see what might be expected of you there.

Case study: Working as a community physiotherapist – Trudy Barr, Band 6 Physiotherapist, Community Response and Rehabilitation Team

I work as part of a wider community multidisciplinary team which aims to prevent hospital admission and to support discharge from hospital. The team includes physiotherapists, occupational therapists, nurses, community psychiatric nurses, podiatrists, specialist therapy assistants and support workers. No day is the same and we receive referrals from a number of different places, including GPs, hospitals, social services, district nurses, and residential and nursing homes. Clients can also refer themselves directly. We will see anyone over the age of 18 who needs the input of more than one of our team. Typical client groups include older people who have had a fall, people with long-term conditions such as Parkinson's disease and also people who have had orthopaedic surgery and have been discharged back into community settings for further rehabilitation.

In the morning I check if any urgent referrals have arrived. We have a rapid response team which has to respond within two hours, so these referrals are a priority. These typically involve clients who are having mobility difficulties and require a detailed moving and handling assessment. If we are unable to resolve the situation or feel that they require hospital admission then we will have to liaise directly with their GP. Frequently we will arrange care packages to support our clients in their own home and prevent them from having to be admitted to hospital, which can be very traumatic for them. Our role is to give clear information to help them make informed decisions and to support them at a very difficult time.

I will also have appointments booked in from previous visits for clients who need further rehabilitation. My treatments could include pain management with the use of acupuncture, electrotherapy such as TENS machines and mobilisation. A large part of my role will be designing exercise programmes and activities to improve my clients' mobility, function and balance in their home and wider environment. I need to ensure that my clients are safe and independent in their own home. This could include providing equipment which could range from a walking stick through to hoists and hospital beds.

I cannot imagine working anywhere but in the community. I get to work with such a diverse group of clients and staff and need to liaise with a variety of agencies such as social care on a daily basis. I get to develop a strong bond with my clients and their families and working in their own home is a privilege. They are much more relaxed in their own home environment than they would be in hospital. You can see directly the challenges that your clients face in their home environment and in collaboration with them you can design a plan to address those problems and see the benefits much more tangibly. You learn to be creative and imaginative in your physiotherapy management and able to deal with some challenging and unpredictable situations. This makes my job very rewarding.

Case study: Amputee and Prosthetic Rehabilitation – Sally Smith

As a Senior Specialist Physiotherapist in Amputee and Prosthetic Rehabilitation, my role is divided between the Physiotherapy Department and the Regional Limb Centre. These are both based at the James Cook University Hospital. My role involves the treatment of inpatients and outpatients from a large geographical area. I assess patients immediately following their surgery and introduce an amputee-specific exercise programme; this is the beginning of their rehabilitation process. Patients are brought to the gym where we carry out exercise programmes, standing and transfer practice. Once the patients are medically fit and safe for discharge, they attend weekly outpatient rehabilitation sessions in preparation for limb wearing. In these sessions patients are trialled with an early walking aid which assists in the decision-making as to whether they are suitable for a prosthesis.

In the Regional Limb Centre I assess patients, alongside the Consultant, for their suitability to wear a prosthesis. Once the patient has had a prosthesis manufactured, I introduce a rehabilitation programme to assist them to mobilise independently, either with or without an appropriate walking aid and practice gait re-education.

Once a patient is walking independently with their prosthesis and is ready for discharge from physiotherapy, I complete a home visit. This is to ensure that the patient is safe in their home environment; the prosthesis is then left with the patient to allow them to mobilise at home.

14: A day in the life – physiotherapy in action

I love my role as a prosthetic physiotherapist as I see patients from admission for surgery through to discharge and becoming independent on their prosthesis. I find my role extremely satisfying and extremely rewarding.

Case study: Working in Women's Health – Maria Ineson, Band 7 Physiotherapist

I work part time every weekday morning and my work is divided between seeing patients in the Outpatient Physiotherapy Department and working on the Maternity and Surgical wards. My ward work involves seeing ladies after they have had a baby, teaching them tummy and pelvic floor exercises and giving them advice to prevent back pain and continence problems following pregnancy and childbirth. On the surgical wards, I teach exercises and give advice to ladies who have had gynaecological surgery such as hysterectomies (removal of the womb), prolapse repairs or continence surgery and to women who have had breast surgery for cancer, to help them in their recovery and in some cases, to help prevent recurrence of the same problems in the future. I also work as part of a multidisciplinary team of doctors, nurses and occupational therapists to ensure that they are able to mobilise and function on discharge and that they have adequate support at home to be safe.

My outpatient work focuses on treating women with musculoskeletal problems in pregnancy such as back, pelvic and wrist pain, through a variety of techniques including exercise, advice, manual therapy (such as massage and joint mobilisation), heat, hydrotherapy (exercise in the water), abdominal braces and supports, acupuncture and TENS therapy (a form of electrical stimulation through the skin and tissues).

In outpatients I also treat women with pelvic floor related problems such as bowel and bladder problems, prolapse and pelvic pain using a variety of techniques such as supervised pelvic floor exercises, pelvic floor stimulation using electrical currents and biofeedback therapy to help improve the quality of life of patients without resorting to surgery. I also treat a small proportion of men with similar problems and see private patients in my own time at a private suite in the hospital at which I am based.

It's a very rewarding job as you can really make improvements to patients' lives. The main personal qualities required are a caring personality with good communication skills. There are lots of opportunities to develop and train further and I am actively involved with the clinical education of students.

Case study: Working in musculoskeletal physiotherapy – David Annison, Senior Specialist Physiotherapist

Within today's modern NHS there are many ways to access and receive care from a musculoskeletal (MSK) physiotherapist. As the title implies, physiotherapists working in this field specialise in the assessment and treatment of the muscular and skeletal systems of the body. MSK physiotherapists often work in teams within departments based in primary, secondary and tertiary care. My role sits within the NHS primary care structure and clinics operate from a small community hospital and two local GP practices.

As a primary care health professional I can receive referrals from local GPs and orthopaedic consultants as well as specialist tertiary care centres for complex problems. Within the locality I also accept self-referrals whereby a patient can contact the department directly to request a physiotherapy appointment. As a first direct contact for patients with an MSK complaint, a high level of knowledge and skill are required to ensure a patient receives safe and effective advice.

My role as a senior specialist physiotherapist means my caseload is varied and can range from simple neck pain, complex fractures and trauma to osteoarthritic joints. The severity of a problem and the speed in which the patient needs to be appointed is generally assessed through information provided on a written referral in a process called triaging, or by direct contact with a consultant etc.

Once triaged, patients will be given an appointment to attend for an assessment of their symptoms. The initial part of an appointment is the subjective assessment, a process whereby a therapist questions the patient about their symptoms to obtain a detailed history or cause for their complaint and a possible diagnosis. The objective assessment will then primarily include a physical examination. This process includes an observation of the area, complex assessment of movement and power, as well as carrying out special specific tests. We also utilise diagnostic imaging such as MRI, diagnostic ultrasound and x-ray to help identify possible causes of pain and symptoms.

Once a working diagnosis has been explained, the patient is informed if their symptoms can be improved with physiotherapy and then given the appropriate advice and treatment. An MSK physiotherapist has many skills at their disposal but frequently uses manual or physical therapies. These include treatments such as massage and stretching, as well as exercise therapy and electrotherapy. My scope of practice also includes advanced skills such as the manipulation of joints and soft tissue, strength and conditioning, and specialised joint and soft tissue injection.

All of the treatments used in daily practice are to help a patient back to their functional and specific goals. For each patient these goals vary and it is therefore important for a physiotherapist working in this field to have a good core knowledge of how the body works in order to tailor treatment plans and exercise programmes.

The scope of an MSK physiotherapist has increased significantly over the last five years and offers an exciting role for any aspiring therapist. My role has developed over the last two years to which I now lead on a telephone physiotherapy advice service that enables patients quicker access to advice within 48 hours of contact. I also now manage a small department and am responsible for their skill development as well as developing my own knowledge and skills in trauma and orthopaedics within accident and emergency. The MSK physiotherapist role continues to expand and the advanced practitioner role is emerging in many care settings. This extended role allows physiotherapists to prescribe medication and carry out interventional procedures, as well as having the responsibility to list patients for surgical procedures. This advanced role has now reached consultant level and highlights an exciting development role for any new physiotherapist within the National Health Service.

Case study: Working in a university – Siobhan Taylor, Senior Lecturer

I am working in a role I never envisaged I would after graduating as a physiotherapist in 1995. It is far removed from the clinical career I held for many years and is in a subject area that is not related to physiotherapy. My title is Senior Lecturer in Service Improvement. I support health and social care students in the development of their leadership skills, personal effectiveness and quality improvement projects.

Whilst working as a physiotherapist I held many roles. I was an adviser to my patients, helping them understand their condition and management options; I was a teacher, delivering educational sessions; I was a supervisor, supporting junior colleagues and students; I was a team member, working collaboratively in a multidisciplinary team; I was a leader, acting as a role model and influencing others to achieve their potential; and I was a manager, heading up physiotherapy services, managing staff, budgets and performance. These roles required a range of transferable skills that I use in my current job. Just like a physiotherapist, the job I hold requires me to work with people from across a range of disciplines, to be an effective team member, to support others' learning and act as a leader. Whilst it may seem evident that these skills are relevant to working as a lecturer, you may wonder where the 'service improvement' element fits in. When I came across the job vacancy it was a surprise to me that, even though my undergraduate degree was not in 'service improvement', I met the employment criteria. Service improvement is something, as a physiotherapist, you are doing all the time. You are assessing the quality of your service provision on a daily basis whilst considering if you are providing the best quality care for your patient. You are undertaking root cause analysis every time you diagnose the reason behind your patients' symptoms. You are analysing data each time you review your patients' progress and amending plans accordingly. These are all key skills related to service improvement and, combined with the leadership skills you draw on to work with your patients and colleagues, you are developing skills that can be transferred across diverse settings and industries. Keep an open mind to your career progression, recognise the transferable skills you have and grasp the opportunities.

Case study: Working with the Olympic team – Julie Sparrow

Seizing opportunities when they present themselves is an essential in life! And a great way to be successful as a physiotherapist in sport.

Three years after qualifying as a physiotherapist I was fortunate to be working with a nurse in an outpatient clinic who was also a gymnastics coach. The town was to open a new gymnastics facility and needed a physio and she asked would I be interested. I went along and the rest as they say is history.

For ten years I worked in gymnastics on a weekly basis looking after the gymnasts, from the tumble tots to the boys who would go on to be international gymnasts. This simple beginning led to the world of sports physiotherapy opening before me and an opportunity to see the world while doing a job I loved.

14: A day in the life – physiotherapy in action

Being part of the GB Olympic team as we marched into the Olympic stadium at the opening ceremony is a moment I will never forget. Watching the flame light and the look of hope and expectation on the faces of the athletes all around me filled me with excitement and fear in equal measure. To work with an Olympic athlete at the pinnacle of their career carries a great responsibility as often this is the one moment in time that will make or break their sporting career.

To get to this point was a journey that demanded long hours of practice and periods of extended study. Of demonstrating to coaches, athletes and performance directors that I had what it takes to cope in the pressure cauldron of sport. Skill levels had to be developed way beyond the basic level I had as I graduated which meant getting experience working across a range of sports. It meant engaging in formal further education and physiotherapy skill-specific courses. It meant learning about the biomechanics of the sports I was working with. Understanding the stresses of travel on the body: jet lag; change of diet; dehydration; travel fatigue; and the impact on performance. Being aware of the psychological demands on the athletes as they trained and peaked for performance.

I have been lucky enough to travel the world but none of it would have been possible without the drive to be the best physiotherapist that I could be. It demanded patience and a commitment to working long hours (the team physiotherapist is often the first up in the morning and the last to bed). The support of peers has also been important and The Association of Chartered Physiotherapists in Sports and Exercise Medicine has been important in providing a forum for support and exchange of ideas.

So what have been the highlights? Being team physio at the World Artistic Gymnastic Championships in France, Australia and Hungary; the World Games in Australia, Finland and Germany; the Commonwealth Games in Malaysia, UK, Australia and India; and the Olympic Games in the US, Australia and London.

A teacher once told me to chase my dreams – I'm still doing it and I love it!

Finally, what will it be like being a student physiotherapist? The following case study gives a brief snapshot of what will be involved.

Case study: A day in the life of a physiotherapy student – Laura Male

Ever since I can remember I have always been interested in physiotherapy and wanted to become a physiotherapist. Many people initially think of physiotherapists just working in sports teams helping players recover from musculoskeletal injuries. However, physiotherapists can be found in a very large range of environments caring for patients who have a range of conditions, such as neurological, musculoskeletal, cardiovascular and respiratory. In the first year I lived in student accommodation with eight other students, of whom all but one were studying something other than physiotherapy. As a healthcare student the hours you spend in university and self-study are much longer than other students. This could be challenging sometimes, but you learn to make the most of time in between lectures to complete notes and pre-reading for lectures later in the week. By learning to use your time sensibly and effectively you don't have to compromise your social life, which for me involved going to the gym and seeing friends.

The BSc Physiotherapy course is full time, Monday to Friday; however, you do spend some of the weekend doing self-study and preparing for lectures the following week. The lectures start at 9am and finish at 4pm every day apart from Wednesday, which is a half day. I found it very useful to get a calendar and write down all of the assignment and exam dates, so I could make sure I gave myself enough time to complete revision and work in order to get the best grades I could.

My normal day at university would begin with only a ten-minute walk to lectures which is one of the bonuses of living in student accommodation on campus! As lectures begin at 9am I would wake up at 8am having already completed any preparation work required for that day and have it ready in my bag the night before. Prior to the lecture I would always print off the PowerPoint slides for the session; this way you make sure you don't have to write as many notes and you have all the information in front of you. Once in class the majority of lectures involve theory and practical aspects, which I found really helpful as you would learn the content then go and practise that skill on your classmates to reinforce the knowledge you have just been taught.

Sometimes you have breaks within the day so I would either go to the library or go home to write up notes from the previous lecture. I could do any other preparation work or further reading that I felt was required. Your days at university are busy and I found that writing up my notes from the lectures every day, whether that was in between lectures or at the end of the day, was really useful. It reinforced the information I had learnt and I made sense of the notes I had scribbled on my print out of the PowerPoint. This was so useful when I was revising and using my notes for assignments.

Chapter summary

The life of a physiotherapist is very varied and, as can be seen from these examples and those throughout this book, there is no one typical day. The demands of practice will require a therapist to draw on the full range of personal attributes to be successful in their work. The common theme throughout these stories is that the service user is at the centre of treatment. Becoming a physiotherapist is an enriching experience which will change lives: not only those you work with but also your own.

Key points

- Take the time to speak to physiotherapists and find out what they do each day.

- If possible look for opportunities to shadow a physiotherapist in order that you can understand more fully the nature of the relationship they have with their clients.

- Try to explore a variety of physiotherapy settings in order that you gain some insight into the breadth of work physiotherapists might be involved in.

Useful resources

NHS Health careers:
www.healthcareers.nhs.uk/explore-roles/allied-health-professionals

Step into the NHS: www.stepintothenhs.nhs.uk/careers

National Careers Service: https://nationalcareersservice.direct.gov.uk

The Chartered Society of Physiotherapy: www.csp.org.uk

Index

Index

Academic skills 11, 74
Accommodation 22, 47, 64
Anatomy 25, 50, 75, 81
Assessment 29, 30

Career paths 107
Charitable sector 9, 13, 110, 135
Chartered Society of
    Physiotherapy 21, 24, 25,
    27, 29, 35, 41, 56, 57, 65,
    73, 111, 112, 147
Communication skills 11, 13, 14,
    27, 37, 74, 85
Continuous professional
    development (CPD) 114
Courses 24, 35

Disclosure and Barring Service
    (DBS) 35
Discovery days 12
Dissertation 29, 66, 97, 99, 103

Eportfolio 101
Erasmus+ exchange 99, 143

Final exams 103
Final year of study 95, 100, 109
Finance 48, 53, 61
Formative assessment 31
Fresher's week 51
Frontline magazine 110

Health and Care Professions
    Council 10, 21, 24, 25, 27,
    35, 73, 97, 101, 111

Independent practice 100, 138
Induction week 51
International working 118
Inter-professional working 13,
    124, 128
Interviews 77

Lectures 15, 31, 78, 80, 85, 117,
    158
Library 49, 52, 65, 76
Listening skills 13, 15, 40, 79

Management 115
Mentorship 109, 113
Modules 29, 31, 97, 99

National Health Service (NHS)
    Knowledge and Skills
    Framework 102, 114
National Student Survey (NSS)
    27, 41, 103
National Union of Students 56

Open days 12
Overseas study 93

Part-time work 56
Personal skills 11, 74, 144
Personal tutor 53, 54, 64, 89,
    101, 103
Physiotherapy 9
Physiotherapy courses 12, 27
Postgraduate programmes 24, 25
Postgraduate Taught Experience
    Survey 41, 103
Practical skills 11, 12, 31, 39, 74
Practice placement 77
    Elective placement 92, 93
    Non-traditional placement 92,
    110
Preceptorship 113
Private practice 133
Problem-based learning (PBL) 30
Professional Code of Conduct
    102
Professional indemnity 113
Professional Standards 90

Research 76, 97, 115

Seminars 79
Standards of Proficiency 90
Statutory sector 121
Student loan 66
Student support 27, 53, 69
Students union 70
Summative assessments 31

Teaching 29, 80
Timetables 48
Transferable skills 26, 80, 143
Tuition fees 53, 66

University and Colleges Admission System (UCAS) 14, 24, 35
University application 35, 69, 103
University interviews 35, 38
University location 21
University reputation 27

Work experience 37
Workshops 81
World Confederation for Physical Therapy 4, 41, 143, 144